DUCHESS OF HAMIL

ULTIMATE IN PACIFIC POW

Michael Blakemore and Michael Rutherford

© M. Blakemore and M. Rutherford, 1990

ISBN 1-872826-00-8

Published by the National Railway Museum, York

Printed by Maxiprint, York

CONTENTS

FRONT COVER: Duchess of Hamilton *storms through Kirkby Stephen, attacking the southbound climb to Ais Gill summit on 11 February 1984. (Paul Stephens)*

46229 leaves a smokescreen over York station as it departs for Scarborough via Hull on Easter Saturday, 6 April 1985. (W. A. Sharman)

THE WEST COAST MAIN LINE

The "Premier Line" at its zenith. No. 2271 J. P. Bickersteth, one of a batch of ten non-superheated "Queen Mary" class 4-4-0s built in 1910 and quickly rebuilt to conform with the superheated "George Vs", is seen being worked hard on the down 2 pm Scottish express — the "Corridor" — near Harrow in 1911. The train is made up of the 1908 twelve-wheeled stock.
(C. Laundy collection/NRM)

The "Princess Coronation" class Pacifics of the London, Midland & Scottish Railway were the most powerful steam locomotives to see service with a British railway company; indeed no production British Railways diesel locomotive could achieve the *peak* horsepower output that these magnificent machines were capable of and that 46229 *Duchess of Hamilton has* produced. There is no doubt that the design could have been further developed to compare with its most advanced contemporaries elsewhere, had there been an operating need or economic justification or, perhaps more realistically, the will to give special treatment to a few hand-picked locomotives for the most prestigious workings.

Unfulfilled potential and performance comparisons will feature later in this book; first, however, we will take a brief look at the history and background of the route (and its problems) that the "Coronations" were built to work over.

The West Coast Route to Scotland is arguably the most romantic of all Britain's great railway routes. It has been immortalised by the poet and the film maker, particularly with regard to one of its most famous trains — one that could be easily idealised by the romantically-minded because it travelled at night and carried no passengers, just fifty busy workers. This was the night Travelling Post Office service known popularly as the "West Coast Postal" or the "Night Mail".

The first unbroken chain of rail communication between London and the two Scottish cities of Glasgow and Edinburgh was completed in February 1848. Fortunately, just one year before, the Trent Valley Railway had opened from Rugby to Stafford, obviating the need for the protracted tour of Birmingham and the Black Country necessary by the original routes of the London & Birmingham and the Grand Junction Railways. The London & Birmingham was the final great civil engineering work that has on it the stamp of George Stephenson and in its execution roots can be traced back to his first railway — that built from Hetton Colliery to the Wear at Sunderland in 1822. There are massive earthworks of cuttings, embankments and tunnels and initially rope haulage out of the Euston terminus was employed. Similarly, at the beginning, the permanent way was "traditional"— short rails chaired onto stone block "sleepers" giving the first passengers a rather bumpy ride in the primitive four-wheeled carriages then employed. The Grand Junction had also been a Stephenson line when construction began but following a row with the "old man", Joseph Locke, his deputy on the project (and a former pupil) took over and the line, which had been authorised by Parliament on the same day as the L & B, opened throughout 15 months earlier than the L & B (at £18,846 per mile as against c£53,000). This gave access from the industrial Midlands to Liverpool and Manchester via the railway company of that name which was absorbed by the GJR in 1845.

The very first train on the line was hauled by a Robert Stephenson "Patentee" type 2-2-2 named *Wildfire,* an excellent contemporary model of which is part of the National Collection at the National Railway Museum. Maintenance of the early locomotives was quite a problem for the locomotive superintendent William Buddicom and in 1840 it was decided to build large new workshops at Crewe, soon to become a very important railway junction and, in 1938, the birthplace of *Duchess of Hamilton.* Buddicom had been developing a locomotive design of his own when the workshops were still at Edge Hill, Liverpool, and this flowered into what is now known as the "Crewe" type, built in many places and used on many railways at home and abroad. An early example of the type is *Columbine,* part of the National Collection and at one time (wrongly) thought to be the first locomotive built at Crewe.

North of the junction with the L & M at Newton Junction near Warrington (long since remodelled and diverted) the West Coast Main Line follows the route of four small companies as far as Lancaster. Here begins another of Locke's great works — the Lancaster & Carlisle Railway which climbs dramatically through the Westmorland fells to the summit at Shap. The line was built cheaply, the notorious Captain Huish demanding that "the projectors...must be satisfied to go *over* the hills, not *through* them... The question of gradients is daily assuming less importance". Locke produced figures to show that the extra fuel needed to traverse such a difficult route would never cost as much as the extra capital needed to engineer an easier line. This, too, was the philosophy with regard to the line north from Carlisle to Glasgow — the Caledonian Railway — which he also engineered and which contains the even more formidable obstacle to steam locomotives of Beattock bank. Part of the reason for this route, which veered east, was to be able to serve Edinburgh as well and this is in fact what happened. Edinburgh and Glasgow portions were united into (or divided from) one train at Carstairs Junction, equidistant from the two cities, and this practice continues to this day.

By 1859 the route between Euston and Carlisle was owned (or leased in the case of the Lancaster & Carlisle until absorbed in 1879) by the London & North Western Railway. The very different terrain in the northern and southern parts demanded different types of locomotive. In the south, McConnell's 2-2-2 type "Bloomers" were the main express locomotives, almost certainly designed by Charles Beyer (later a founding partner of Beyer-Peacock & Co.) who was chief designer at Sharp, Roberts & Co., the builders of the first batch in 1851. These engines featured inside plate frames and inside cylinders; they were clean of line and ran well and fast. Further north, the original "Crewe" type was still the standard together with John Ramsbottom's "Problem" or "Lady of the Lake" class, 7'6" express "Singles" derived from the "Crewe" type but without the extra reinforcing framing around the cylinders and thus inside bearings on the carrying wheels. The Lancaster & Carlisle also used the "Crewe" type, many being supplied by the LNWR under the terms of the lease.

In Scotland the Caledonian's locomotive superintendent Benjamin Connor introduced some 2-2-2 locomotives with 8'2" driving wheels and "Crewe" framing but with horizontal cylinders (reminiscent of the unique LNWR *Cornwall* as rebuilt in 1858 and also a member of the National Collection). In spite of these massive wheels, they performed very well on Beattock with express trains and ran like the wind elsewhere, mainly due to excellent valve events including a lap of 1¼" in conjunction with long travel. This enabled the exhaust side of the piston to remain open to exhaust longer, after the incoming steam on the other side had been "cut-off" and allowed to expand, thus preventing excess compression and back pressure. Unfortunately Connor's successor, Drummond, modified all this for reasons best known to himself and they ceased to perform nearly so well, although by that time their boilers were too small for current needs.

The simplicity of the inside plate frames and inside cylinders of the "Bloomers" gradually became the norm at Crewe under Ramsbottom, Webb (apart from his Compounds) and Whale, as well as at St. Rollox on the Caledonian under Drummond, Lambie and McIntosh. Webb's 2-4-0 *Hardwicke* (preserved at the NRM) ran the 141 miles from Crewe to Carlisle in 126 minutes in the "Races to the North" of 1895, averaging 60.4 mph from Carnforth to Shap Summit (admittedly with a very light load.)

The competition with the East Coast Route that resulted in the "Races" turned more to a competition for amenities than for speed after 1896 and an agreement to fix the timing at 8¼ hours from Euston to Glasgow had been made. This was probably just as well because in July 1893 the 2 pm Glasgow express departure (first introduced in 1889) became the first LNWR express train to consist of corridor stock throughout. Thus it became known to railway staff and public alike as the "Corridor". It carried both First and Third Class restaurant facilities; there were, in fact, two composite restaurant cars, one in each of the Glasgow and Edinburgh portions. The 1908 set of new twelve-wheeled carriages (the restaurant cars were not new) was one of the finest sets of stock ever used in normal service on any railway in this country. The quality of workmanship in these vehicles can be judged from the surviving vehicles of the LNWR Royal Train, preserved at the National Railway Museum; although slightly earlier in vintage the construction is to the same high standard. By 1914 the LNWR, the biggest joint stock company in the world and the biggest (and busiest!) railway company in the United Kingdom, had undoubtedly earned the right to call itself "The Premier Line".

A snowy day on Shap as 46229 climbs towards the summit on 8 February 1960. (Derek Cross)

LONDON, MIDLAND AND SCOTTISH

The Railway Act of 1921, grouping the railway companies into the "Big Four" in 1923, was not due to any political pressure as was nationalisation in 1948 but was a business strategy to help get the railways back on their feet following the Great War. It was accepted with apprehensive caution in most railway circles, being regarded as unnecessary and not the best possible solution. There was no doubt that some grouping should take place and in the year of the Act the London & North Western Railway amalgamated with one of its northern competitors, the Lancashire & Yorkshire Railway, under circumstances of mutual friendliness. The forced amalgamation at the Grouping with the Midland Railway was far from friendly and was to cause considerable problems on the newly-created London, Midland & Scottish Railway for at least a decade.

That a much smaller company than the LNWR should gain the upper hand in the new organisation may at first seem surprising. However, the senior ranks of the LNWR had been severely diminished by retirements (the Chairman, Sir Gilbert Claughton, for example) and deaths (in particular those of Sir Guy Calthrop, the General Manager, and Charles Bowen-Cooke, the Chief Mechanical Engineer and organiser of the prodigious arms production at Crewe throughout the war). It was, to use the words of the late Hamilton Ellis, "that wily old lawyer Sir William Guy Granet, sometime Dictator of the Midland" whose Machiavellian tactics were to win the day. O. S. Nock summed it up admirably in *LMS Steam:* "Behind locked doors, as it were, the men of the enlarged North Western and no less those of the Scottish companies had, long before that fateful January of 1923, felt the well-nigh impregnable strength of Midland high management and particularly the personality of Sir Guy Granet. Step by step, inexorably he virtually dictated the terms of amalgamation and, although he did not become either chairman or deputy chairman of the new company, he dominated the proceedings of the board . . . The result was that Midland precepts of management were adopted for the new company. Seventeen years earlier Granet had completely overthrown the traditional form of railway organisation which had prevailed on the Midland as firmly as on all the other large railways of Great Britain, and now it was the turn of the other constituents of the LMS to experience what the Midland had passed through from 1906 onwards".

The operating plank of the new structure was Centralised Traffic Control (CTC), a system designed to increase the efficiency of traffic movement at the same time as reducing operating costs. It was first tried on the lines between Toton and Leeds which were severely congested with freight traffic. Enginemen could be on duty for extremely long periods (and relief crews likewise) without turning a wheel. To match men, locomotives, wagons and the rest to operating requirements and timetables was the job of the various district control offices connected by a vast network of telephones and co-ordinated with a complex system of forms, coloured cards, tickets, charts and graphs. The whole complicated arrangement was a complete success but it masked many problems in the locomotive department; these problems were exacerbated by time and re-emerged in early LMS days when the system was forced onto the ex-LNWR lines and particularly onto the operations on the West Coast Main Line.

Under the new scheme the Midland had classified its locomotives in power classes 1, 2, 3 and 4. Each class was given a load restriction which was not to be exceeded without the assistance of a pilot engine. This meant that the limit was set by the least efficient engine within this nominal power class. In reality, some locomotives could haul substantially heavier loads but were not allowed to do so and were compelled to take a pilot. The Midland was noted for a "small engine policy" which was to be read in conjunction with frequent light trains in passenger service. The idea of running light frequent Scottish expresses with full facilities was, of course, absurd and an attempt to mask the Board's (i.e. Granet's) skinflint policy with regard to locomotive development. R. M. Deeley, who was locomotive superintendent at Derby from 1904 to 1909, was continually frustrated in introducing up-to-date designs; his eight-coupled freight locomotive was quashed and a four-cylinder compound express passenger locomotive dismissed on the grounds of excessive development costs. He finally resigned towards the end of 1909; he was a great loss to a profession to which he never returned but continued to make his name in many other scientific fields.

On most railways locomotive running, sheds and footplate staff were all part of the chief mechanical engineering department; in the Midland system these functions and personnel became a responsibility of the general manager's department — indeed the CME could not board a footplate without permission! The LNWR had 505 superheated express passenger engines to contribute to the LMS, including 130 "Claughton" class four-cylinder 4-6-0s. Although banking trains out of Euston, from Tebay to Shap and on Beattock bank was normal, double-heading was not, except in extreme cases or to work an engine home. It was standard practice on the LNWR to flog engines mercilessly if necessary to keep heavy trains to time, even at the expense of high coal consumption which, before the war, was so low in price as to cause no serious concern. The introduction of Midland methods caused double-heading to become the norm all along the WCML and this resulted in footplate crews leaving it to the other engine to do all the work and showing a complete reluctance to "have a go". All this was now out of the hands of the CME's department.

The amalgamation of the LYR in 1921 led to that company's CME, George Hughes, based at Horwich, becoming the new overall CME of the North Western due to seniority. On the formation of the LMS in 1923 he again took the senior position, with Horwich becoming briefly a fount of new ideas in locomotive design. The new LMS Motive Power Department, however, was set up at Derby under J. H. Follows, the Chief Operating Officer, a Midland man and chief expert on CTC. The CME had, in theory, an input into this department, but in practice this was not the case as the representative (Chief of Motive Power) was J. E. Anderson, another Midland man and believer in the old ways (known as "the dead hand of Derby" elsewhere) who killed all attempts at Horwich to produce large modern locomotives.

Hughes' deputy was H. E. O'Brien who was also the manager of Horwich, well-educated and of "private means". He had been in charge of the LYR's pioneer electrification work under John Aspinall and later became Electrical Engineer of the LMS. In this capacity he set up a new section at Horwich and began to scheme a proposal to electrify the Crewe-Carlisle section of the WCML. In 1924 O'Brien read a paper to the Institute of Electrical Engineers entitled "The Future of Main Line Electrification on British Railways" and cited WCML as an example. This public heresy caused a good deal of fluttering in the Euston dovecotes of the new LMS management and O'Brien was summoned to explain himself. Unwilling to repent and unable to agree with the new regime and progress his plans, he "resigned" and retired to his estates in Ireland.

Georges Hughes has been somewhat under-rated in locomotive history; he was an excellent workshop man and did much in the way of testing and experimental work, including road testing of locomotives with a fully-equipped dynamometer car. He must, however, shoulder the blame for 20 non-puissant 4-cylinder 4-6-0s built at Horwich in 1908/9. The design work was in the hands of Zachariah Tetlow, Chief Draughtsman since the opening of Horwich in 1887 and clearly getting out of his depth with contemporary practice. One was rebuilt after the Great War, with outside Walschaerts valve gear and piston valves instead of the inside Joy gear and slide valves of the earlier version. This rebuild was successful and more were put in hand, including new engines to the modified design. A little later, the drawings were resuscitated of a 1914 scheme for a 4-cylinder 2-10-0 which had been influenced by Flamme's massive 4-cylinder 2-10-0s and 4-6-2s in Belgium, a country which Hughes visited in 1911.

The need for new express passenger locomotives on the WCML in early LMS days became clearer as the months went by. The LNWR locomotives were heavy on coal and costly in maintenance and the Midland small engine policy seemed inappropriate to the "Corridor" and the rest. Few of the other constituent companies had much to offer except, surprisingly, the Highland Railway. Perhaps the best of a number of excellent designs built by the Newcastle firm of Hawthorn, Leslie & Co. were the "River" class 4-6-0s of F. G. Smith. An internal HR dispute resulted in Smith's dismissal and the locomotives never actually turned a revenue-earning wheel on the Highland but they were sold (at a tidy profit!) to the Caledonian Railway whose own new designs at St. Rollox were "missing the mark", although in 1913, just before he retired, McIntosh had a couple of Pacifics drawn up (one with a wide firebox of 37 sq. ft., the other with a narrow one of 27 sq. ft.), both with four cylinders.

With Pacifics appearing on the East Coast Main Line in 1922 (Nigel Gresley's on the Great Northern and Sir Vincent Raven's on the North Eastern), it was natural that the CME of the LMS should be thinking in a similar vein and a four-cylinder layout was derived from the rebuilt 4-6-0s. A freight 2-8-2 was also proposed using the same boiler and cylinders. The Derby conventicle evinced some interest in the 2-8-2 for the Toton-Brent coal traffic but asked for three cylinders instead of four. The Pacific was likewise re-schemed. Derby also at about this time proposed a much-enlarged three-cylinder compound of the 4-6-0 type.

Hughes retired in 1925 and was succeeded by Sir Henry Fowler. Applied Science was Fowler's forté and his subject was metallurgy; it is said that he happily admitted to never having designed a locomotive in his life. He was thus something of a pawn of the operating department as far as new locomotives were concerned and his manifestation in the Works in full Boy Scout uniform did little to inspire confidence in certain quarters of the drawing office!

With the departure of Hughes, the 4-6-2 and 2-8-2 schemes were altered to become compounds but reverted to a four-cylinder layout; serious work began on the design side and one of the Hughes 4-6-0s (of recent build) was rebuilt into a compound - the most modern compound ever run by a British railway company. Meanwhile, the operating department had flooded the system with large numbers of a re-vamped Midland design of the three-cylinder compound 4-4-0. They decided to divide the heavy WCML expresses into two portions with one of these engines on each. They soon found that once into the fell country north of Carnforth they were having to put two on each portion. Four engines were thus required to do the work that a LNWR "Claughton" or a well-flogged "George V" 4-4-0 were proven to be capable of in pre-grouping days.

As work on Fowler's compound Pacific proceeded — design work at Derby, materials ordered (and delivered, it is said) at Crewe — the Motive Power Department in the shape of Follows and Anderson became worried, seeing much expense in new 65 ft. or 70 ft. turntables and much trouble in familiarisation of crews with massive new machines potentially full of unknown troubles. So it was that they went to the very top of the LMS hierarchy and persuaded the Company to ask the Great Western Railway for the loan of one of its "Castle" class 4-6-0s, modest in size but already with a formidable reputation.

In September 1926 No. 5000 *Launceston Castle* appeared at Euston for tests with the dynamometer car. E. S. Cox, who was present for the tests, has written: "Throughout the whole exercise No. 5000 performed with quiet mastery all the work on which the 'Claughtons', often piloted, lost time, dropped their steam pressure and made the welkin ring with their reverberating exhaust. It displayed the full measure of the extent to which Bowen-Cooke had failed to absorb the lesson of the earlier GW-LNW locomotive exchange in 1910, which was the forerunner of the 'Claughton' design''. This is a little unfair on Cox's part; ex-works the "Claughtons" were extremely good machines and most technical problems were of a minor nature and were easily solved (but too late). They were, however, difficult to fire, there being two different designs of grate and firemen could not get away with simply "baling it in".

Nevertheless in October 1926 "the word" reached Derby and all work on the compound Pacific stopped abruptly. Apparently the GWR had been approached to build 50 "Castles" for the LMS but this request was refused as was that for a set of drawings. Private industry was therefore consulted in the shape of the North British Locomotive Company of Glasgow which undertook to construct 50 three-cylinder 4-6-0s, initially referred to as "Improved Castles". The first of these engines — No. 6100 *Royal Scot* — was delivered in August 1927, the design work having been done in Glasgow although drawings of Derby practice were sent for incorporation where possible. Perhaps this is what the Midland operating men had always wanted — something bought in, just as American railroads would have gone to Alco or Baldwins, cutting out inter-departmental jealousies and avoiding the provincial industrial empires inherited from the great Victorian locomotive superintendents. Anyway, they had their engines; they certainly were not the last word but at least they could deal with the normal WCML load of anything up to fifteen carriages without incessant double-heading.

In May 1925 the LMS Board had announced the creation of a new office, that of President of the Executive. He, together with four Vice-Presidents, would form an Executive Committee. To the position of President in January 1926 came Sir Josiah Charles Stamp (later Lord Stamp). Stamp came to be virtually dictator of the LMS, having total executive control and he resolved that the inherited conflicts between the various factions of the locomotive and operating departments would have to cease once and for all and thus there could be no question of a new CME being appointed from any of the warring bands of Crewe, Derby, Horwich and St. Rollox. H. P. M. Beames at Crewe, who had been the last CME of the mighty LNWR before the amalgamation with the LYR, was to be left out in the cold yet again. Stamp would not consider a North Western man under any circum-stances and is reported to have remarked "If I make an old London & North Western man CME, Crewe will have a banquet with fireworks afterwards".

In 1931 Fowler was made a Vice-President and E. H. Lemon became CME briefly as a stop-gap measure while Stamp looked for a suitable "outsider".

WILLIAM STANIER TO THE RESCUE

William Stanier (NRM)

Josiah Stamp, who was himself an economist and a notable statistician, had a great reverence for Science and his Presidential Address to the Institute of Transport in 1929 was entitled *Scientific Research in Transport.* Little wonder, then, that early in 1930 Sir Harold Hartley CBE FRS, a Balliol don, became Vice-President (Works and Ancilliary Undertakings) and Director of Scientific Research of the LMS. It was Hartley who "set-up" William Stanier by using E. H. Lemon to invite him (Stanier) to dine at the Athenaeum Club. Stanier had known Lemon for some years; there was much discussion about water softening and a second meeting was arranged at which Hartley offered Stanier the CME post, including control of the running department.

For most of his working life William Arthur Stanier had been a Great Western man; indeed he always averred that "I have got GWR embroidered on the seat of my trousers!" He was born in Swindon on 27 May 1876, the year in which the GWR absorbed the South Devon Railway and with it acquired the services of Stanier's future boss and mentor, George Jackson Churchward.

Stanier's father, William Henry, spent over fifty years in the service of the GWR, beginning in the office of William Dean when the latter was Works Manager at Wolverhampton, at that time headquarters of the Northern Division under Joseph Armstrong. When Sir Daniel Gooch retired from the position of Locomotive Superintendent of the GWR in 1864, Armstrong moved down to Swindon and Dean was promoted at Wolverhampton. Stanier Senior moved down to the Wiltshire town in 1871 to work for Dean who had followed Armstrong as his Chief Assistant in 1868.

Gooch's office had been in the railway's headquarters at Paddington and the "New Town" at Swindon had similarities with the American "Wild West". It was Joseph Armstrong who, by building himself a large residence near the Works (named "Newburn" after his birthplace on the River Tyne), attending to the needs of the men under him, and involving himself deeply in civic duties, transformed Swindon into an ordered and growing community.

Stanier Senior also played an important part in local affairs, being active in many of the organisations for railway staff as well as serving as a councillor and alderman for a number of years and becoming Mayor for the year 1908/9. His major achievement, however, was in his commitment to the education of the young, both at school and as apprentices. From being William Dean's Chief Clerk, he was promoted to Stores Superintendent in 1892 and held that post until 1915 when he became Assistant to the General Manager of the GWR at Paddington.

It was also in 1892, in the final months of the Broad Gauge, that his son took up an apprenticeship at Swindon. After completing his apprenticeship, he served as a draughtsman for two years before going to Birmingham for two months as Inspector of Materials. In 1901 Stanier was appointed Technical Inspector at Swindon running shed and in 1903 was promoted to Assistant Divisional Superintendent, Swindon. The following year he went in a similar capacity to Paddington, during a hectic period when the London sheds were in the process of moving from the cramped site at Westbourne Park to Old Oak Common. Throughout this time Stanier gained valuable experience of locomotive running from the ground.

He returned to Swindon in 1906 as Divisional Locomotive Superintendent and held that position until 1913 when he was appointed Chief Assistant to the Works Manager at Swindon, succeeding to the Works Managership in January 1920. He thus had all-round locomotive experience when, in January 1924, he was made Principal Assistant to the Chief Mechanical Engineer, C. B. Collett. Like his father, Stanier took a wide interest in the affairs of Swindon and did, in fact, represent Collett (who was somewhat reclusive in these matters) at most social functions. In 1927 the GWR decided to send a number of exhibits to the Baltimore & Ohio Railroad Centenary celebrations, including No. 6000 *King George V* and the replica broad gauge *North Star,* and Stanier had the privilege of accompanying the locomotives to America.

Stanier was only five years younger than Collett and, as his deputy, could only expect a short reign as CME himself, assuming that Collett retired at the normal age (which in the event he didn't). Although he was perfectly happy to remain in this position, when Sir Harold Hartley of the LMS twice invited him to lunch, it soon became clear that he was being offered a unique opportunity and a great challenge.

Collett and other senior GWR men gave him the "green light" and there is no doubt that Churchward, Great Western locomotive chief from 1902 to 1921 and who had remained in "Newburn" after his retirement, afforded him a good deal of advice and encouragement.

Stamp wished Stanier to replace the vast and diverse multitude of run-down and out-dated locomotives by a lesser number of high-availability standard types — a strategy based on Churchward's approach on the GWR. The workshops were also to be re-organised on the lines of that carried out at Crewe under the indomitable Captain Beames who wrote a letter to Stanier on his appointment that included the words "There is no-one I would rather serve under than you". At last, at senior level the feuding was at an end although Stamp was never able to produce an organisation to which the majority of rank and file staff

felt any loyalty and he himself was generally feared; appearances of his special saloon on tours of inspection in remote corners of the system were regarded as "sacking jaunts", as they often turned out to be.

Stanier's great experience was in the running side and the workshops; he had received little drawing office experience and was no designer of engines. It should not be thought, therefore, that the existing drawing office staff were incapable of appreciating up-to-date techniques and practice; indeed the two-cylinder 2-6-4 passenger tank engines introduced in Fowler's time, with their 10″ long-travel piston valves with 1¼″ lap which produced locomotives that ran like the wind, showed that, given the chance, Derby drawing office was as good as anywhere. It should also be remembered that 245 of Hughes' Horwich-designed class 5 2-6-0s (the "Crabs") were doing solid work all over the LMS system - the first example of this type, No. 2700, survives in the National Collection.

A large passenger locomotive for the WCML expresses was still a pressing priority and one of

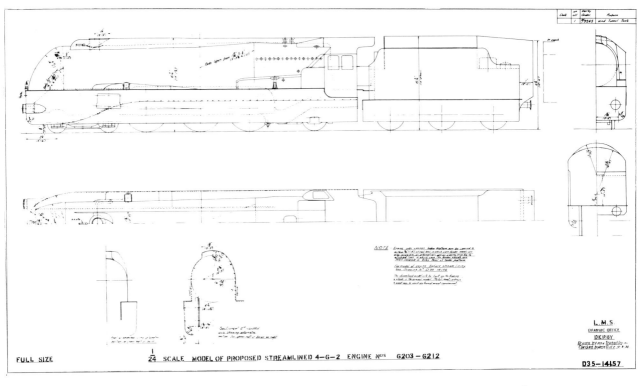

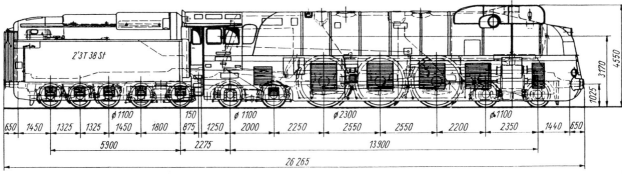

A drawing of the first LMS streamlining proposal — as used in a wind tunnel model — shown with a diagram of the Reichsbahn 05 class 4-6-4, obviously its inspiration.

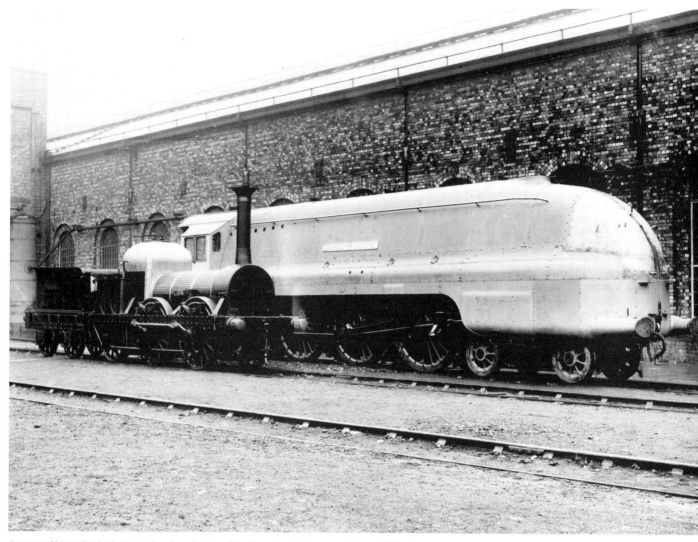

A century of locomotive development: a brand-new Duchess of Hamilton *alongside the veteran Liverpool & Manchester Railway* Lion *outside Crewe Works on 25 August 1938.*
(National Railway Museum)

Stanier's earliest tasks was to decide on which was the most suitable between two 4-6-2s then proposed, one with the three-cylinder layout of the "Royal Scots" and the other having the four-cylinder layout of the GWR "Stars", "Castles" and "Kings" with which Stanier was familiar. Three engines of the latter design were initially ordered but the third was held back to become a non-condensing turbine locomotive (using parts standard with the other two wherever possible). This arose from Stanier's visit to the Grangeberg-Oxelösund Railway in Sweden in 1932. Stanier was impressed by his inspection and by the enthusiasm of Dr. Henry Guy of Metro-Vickers who supplied the turbine gear for what was to become LMS No. 6202, known as the "Turbomotive".

The first two of Stanier's Pacifics, Nos. 6200 and 6201, were a combination of the GWR 4-6-2 *The Great Bear* and the "King" 4-6-0s, together with details arrived at in work on Fowler's stillborn Pacific of 1925. Delivered in 1933, they proved at first to be poor steamers due to badly worked-out internal boiler dimensions and ratios, while Stanier was reported to have been somewhat displeased with their overall finish. No more were ordered until the following year when a further ten were authorised for construction in 1935.

Boilers of a modified design were built with a larger firebox volume, achieved by the incorporation of a combustion chamber which in turn reduced the length between the tubeplates. A bigger superheater was specified but, with an even larger one being provided for the turbine engine, this latter design was embodied in the last six of the order for the ten locomotives Nos. 6203-6212. There were other detail alterations and the first two examples were eventually brought into line. These Pacifics (the "Princess Royals") were now very fine machines capable of heavy haulage and high speeds; on 3 May 1936 No. 6203 *Princess Margaret Rose* reached 102.5 mph during a series of brake tests.

A further five engines (Nos. 6213-6217) were approved in July 1936 for the 1937 construction programme but a decision was then taken by the LMS to introduce a new streamlined express and to modify these locomotives accordingly. However, T. F. Coleman, Stanier's Technical Assistant and Chief Draughtsman at Derby, suggested more drastic redesign, his submission being that a much larger and and more powerful locomotive was possible. It is to Stanier's eternal credit that, rather than stick to the now reliable "Princesses" but with a fashionable new exterior, he was prepared to allow more — possibly speculative — expense in design work and so was born the "Coronation" class. His faith in Coleman's team was not misplaced and the final product came to be regarded as Stanier's masterpiece. When in May 1937 the first of the new locomotives, No. 6220 appropriately named *Coronation,* was publicly unveiled at Crewe Works in its dramatic streamlining and arrayed in an arresting blue livery with silver bands, the press handout stated that it was "designed by the Drawing Office staffs at Crewe and Derby" rather than naming the CME. This was a generous touch from Stanier and it is difficult to imagine a similar gesture emanating from many other CMEs.

T. F. ("Tommy") Coleman had served an apprenticeship with Kerr Stuart & Co. of Stoke-on-Trent from 1900 to 1906 when he moved to the North Staffordshire Railway as Works Plant Draughtsman, while earlier in his career he had found time to turn out for Stoke City in the Football League. At the Grouping in 1923, Coleman was Chief Draughtsman on the NSR but in 1926 Fowler closed some of the smaller offices, including Stoke, and Coleman transferred to Horwich in the same capacity.

With the advent of the Stanier regime, Horwich designed a two-cylinder taper-boiler 2-6-0 and Coleman was quick to catch Stanier's eye. In 1933 he moved to Crewe as Chief Draughtsman of both Crewe and Horwich and did much of the spadework for the "Black Five" 4-6-0 and the "8F" 2-8-0. Coleman went on to assemble a good team including a number of men from the private locomotive-building industry such as L. Barraclough (ex-N.B. Loco. Co. who had worked on the LNER "Sandringhams") and G. R. Nicholson (ex-Yorkshire Engine Co.), plus D. Willcocks from Horwich and J. Francis, the best of the home-grown Crewe draughtsmen. Two men already at Derby at this time, E. S. Cox (ex-Horwich) and E. A. Langridge, have written fascinating and detailed reminiscences of this period. It was little wonder, bearing in mind the teething troubles that had been experienced with some of the Derby designs for Stanier, that in March 1935 Coleman should have been given the task of finally co-ordinating all the design work and eliminating any last remnants of out-dated practices and inter-company rivalry.

On the rival East Coast Line, the London & North Eastern Railway had consistently sought to improve its Anglo-Scottish passenger traffic by publicity-attracting innovations such as the non-stop "Flying Scotsman" service as early as 1928. The streamlined "Silver Jubilee" service in 1935 headed by Gresley's eye-catching "A4" class locomotives was regarded by the LMS as a publicity stunt and, as it only ran to Newcastle, was not considered as a commercial threat. But in the autumn of 1936 when the LNER announced its intention of introducing a streamlined high-speed train between London and Edinburgh in 1937, Coronation year, the LMS decided that *it* must have a suitable response ready — and it must be a streamlined one.

Although the streamlining fad in the USA had more to do with style than substance, there was a genuine attempt in Europe to quantify the possible fuel savings and performance improvements that applied aerodynamics could bring to locomotives and trains. Nowhere was this carried out more meticulously than in Germany, initially with high-speed diesel trains and then with steam locomotives, notably with a pair of huge three-cylinder 4-6-4s with 7'6" driving wheels which were capable of speeds up to 120 mph fairly effortlessly and one of which then held the world speed record of 124.5 mph made on 11 May 1936. During that same year Stanier himself, during a visit to Germany by the Institution of Locomotive Engineers, travelled on the footplate at 118 mph. The equivalent of "chief mechanical engineer" on the Reichsbahn was Richard P. Wagner who read a number of papers to the I. Loco. E. in London, and the German method of boiler calculations was adopted in many quarters in Britain, including the LMS, although some features of design were not.

Josiah Stamp was also very familiar with Germany, having been the British representative in the Reparations Commission's 1924 Committee on German currency and finance which initiated the formation of the Deutsches Reichsbahn-Gesellschaft (German State Railway Company) under Dr. Julius Dorpmüller. The DRG's dozen or so years of autonomy, before succumbing to take-over by the Nazi state apparatus, showed almost miraculous progress in all departments and services and undoubtedly coloured Stamp's view of the direction the LMS should take. His links with many of the most senior members of the Nazi government caused a number of unfortunate incidents but his death by German bombs in a wartime air-raid, although tinged with irony, was a great loss to the LMS.

Aerodynamics and wind tunnels were an ideal field for Hartley's Scientific Research Department and a wind tunnel was installed in the new laboratories at Derby, where various locomotive models were subjected to streams of air and measurements. In some ways these were a continuation of tests carried out at the National Physical Laboratory by F. C. Johansen a year or so earlier. The outcome was that the streamlined shape proposed for the "Coronations" was, not unnaturally, very similar to that of the Reichsbahn locomotives.

Now Coleman had two major ideas for the new batch of Pacifics: to eliminate the two inside sets of valve gear of the "Princess Royals" and to fit the largest

The LMS poster by Bryan de Grineau for the new "Coronation Scot" service in 1937, showing the first blue streamlined style. (National Railway Museum)

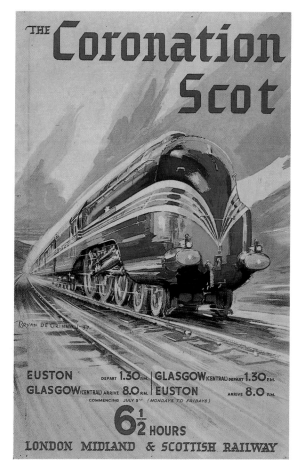

The streamlined Pacifics made excellent subjects for publicity posters. This one by Rethi, showing locomotives under construction, was also issued in 1937. (National Railway Museum).

T. F. Coleman (NRM)

possible diameter boiler with increased diameter driving wheels. Four diagrams were prepared as follows:

Diagram No.	Description	Estimated Weights: Engine only, in working order
ED 255	"Princess Royal" with shortened coupled wheelbase (7'3" + 7'3") and outside cylinders moved forward 9"	104t 0cwt
ED 258	"Princess Royal" as above but with inclined inside cylinders, GWR-type rocking gear worked from outside, larger diameter boiler and shorter firebox (8'0"). Possibly 9" piston valves envisaged at this stage.	105t 0cwt
ED 259	As above but with 8'6" long firebox — and therefore bigger grate area.	105t 16cwt
ED 260	Streamlined but still with footplate, driving wheels 6'9", cylinder/rocking gear layout as on LYR 4-6-0s	106t 0cwt
ED 261	Non-streamlined version of above	105t 5cwt

Although there had been a drawing made for a streamlined "Princess" model for wind tunnel tests, ED 260 was the only streamlined diagram prepared. Coleman is supposed to have taken two alternative diagrams to Euston to obtain Stanier's approval before the CME left for India on a Committee of Enquiry and he certainly knew how to present his case. Both schemes (ED 259 and 260) had a larger boiler but the most radically modified cylinder layout is included on the diagram with larger wheels and streamlining, the latter demanded by the Company. David Jenkinson has related how R. A. Riddles (formerly Stanier's principal assistant) told him that Stanier had said, with regard to the request for streamlining, "I have decided it is better

to please a fool than tease him; they can have their bloody streamliners if they want them but we will build five proper ones as well!"

So Coleman got through all his modifications on the back of streamlining. It would, however, be interesting to know how he justified an estimated 106 tons only for all-up engine weight as the first LMS 4-6-2 had scaled 111t 8cwt instead of an estimated 103t 15cwt. In the event the streamlined engine came out at 108t 2cwt, which was quite good as the streamlining was an unknown quantity in many respects. Much weight was saved by the use of alloy steels and remarkably full details appeared in the *Railway Gazette.*

The first batch of five engines was put to work in June and July 1937. No. 6220 *Coronation* was soon in the news with a speed of 114 mph on a demonstration run from Euston to Crewe on 29 June 1937, averaging 80 mph on the return journey of which 69.9 miles were at an average of 87.4 mph.

The new train, the "Coronation Scot" commenced running in the summer timetable, departing Euston at 1.30 pm for Glasgow only. The old 2 pm "corridor" service (officially named the "Midday Scot" in 1927) was revamped to provide Edinburgh passengers only with a restaurant car service. The train was re-marshalled at Carlisle with the addition of a Manchester-Edinburgh portion and the dividing of the Glasgow portion from the train.

The following batch of ten locomotives, part of the 1938 construction programme, was built as five streamlined and five non-streamlined to ED 261. A water-tube firebox was planned for one of these engines but this was not proceeded with, perhaps due to Stanier departing again for India on another Committee of Enquiry. André Chapelon had published his famous *La Locomotive à Vapeur* in 1938 and his advocacy of internal streamlining of the steam passages resulted in new cylinder and piston valve drawings being prepared but it is not clear if this particular design was ever used as the numbers of the engines selected have been erased from the drawings. What *is* certain, however, is that Nos. 6234 *Duchess of Abercorn* and 6229 *Duchess of Hamilton* were definitely built with a new design of cylinder. No. 6229 was, in fact, held back on the production line for this purpose and was the last engine of the batch to enter traffic. The late C. Williams, who meticulously recorded the happenings at Crewe, wrote in one of his notebooks "Minute 1176, 21/4/38. 4-6-2 Engines. E1108 Account. All shops to note the No. 5 frame (i.e. No. 6229) is to be fitted with streamlined cylinders; this being so it will be necessary for No. 5 frame to be dropped out of sequence and Nos. 6, 7, 8, 9 and 10 brought forward. No. 5 will therefore be the last engine completed. . . . It is to be noted that engines 6229 and 6234 will be fitted with the new pattern cylinders, drop grates and hopper ashpans".

46229 — THE STORY OF A LOCOMOTIVE

Following the success of the first five "Coronation" Pacifics introduced in 1937, a further batch of ten was authorised for the 1938 construction programme of which Nos. 6225-6229 were again to be streamlined, but this time the blue and silver finish which had proved so striking was replaced by an even more magnificent maroon and gold livery. All ten were designated after duchesses of the realm (so giving the title by which the class was often known) and locomotive No. 6229 was duly accorded the name *Duchess of Hamilton*.

The Hamiltons are one of Scotland's foremost families, the dukedom having been created by Charles I in 1643. However, the wife of James Hamilton, the first Duke, had died before the award of the title so initially there was no Duchess and James suffered the further misfortune, following his army's defeat by Cromwell, of being beheaded for "invading England in a hostile manner" in support of the King. As he left no heir, the title passed to his brother William whose wife Elizabeth became the first Duchess of Hamilton in 1649.

No. 6229 *Duchess of Hamilton* was completed at Crewe Works on 7 September 1938 at a cost (including tender) of £11,302. After a couple of days tests and trials, it was sent to Crewe North depot where it officially entered service on 10 September but hardly had the engine settled down to work when a major upheaval in its brief career took place.

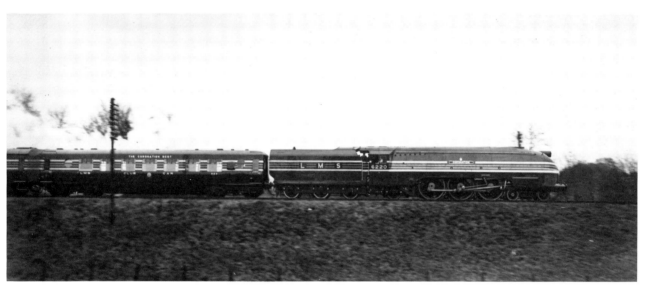

Now carrying the name and number 6220 Coronation *for its American tour, the locomotive is seen on a test run at King's Langley on 9 January 1939.*
(The Photo Source/Keystone Press Agency Ltd.)

An Ambassador to America

To mark the 150th anniversary of the inauguration of George Washington as President of the USA, a huge "exposition" (claimed to be the biggest in history) was planned to be staged in New York in 1939 with the aim of showing "the way toward the improvement of all the factors contributing to human welfare". Covering a total of 1,216 acres, with sixty nations participating and representing an investment of almost $150,000,000, the World's Fair was expected to draw over 50 million visitors and the Railroad Exhibit, itself occupying 17 acres, was to be the largest individual feature of the spectacle. As well as enormous models and dioramas demonstrating the construction and operation of American railroads, over 4,500 ft. of track were to be dedicated to a display of the very latest in American and European trains.

The Americans had shown considerable interest in the "Coronation Scot" and in October 1937 the LMS accepted an invitation to send one of its trains to the World's Fair. However, the Chief Operating Manager felt it would be difficult to spare vehicles for a prolonged visit overseas and so it was decided to exhibit a completely new train composed of three twin-articulated sets, augmented by a modern twelve-wheel sleeping car and a club saloon. The latter two were not to be part of the "Coronation Scot" in normal service but were included to show off other aspects of LMS coachbuilding; the sleeping car would have the added advantage of affording accommodation for staff during the tour. The train, with additional vehicles not constructed in the time available, was to enter traffic on the LMS in 1940, accompanied by two similar new trains.

The locomotive selected to head the train was the newest member of the "Coronation" class, No. 6229. As previously mentioned, this engine was the last of the

1938 batch to be completed, and it could well be that 6229 had been marked down for the tour at an early stage.

Duchess of Hamilton thus returned on 9 December to Crewe Works where it exchanged names and numbers with the original member of the class, No. 6220 *Coronation,* the LMS having decided that this should be the name carried by the locomotive visiting America. Various trappings, such as a headlamp, bell, spark arrestor and automatic coupler, were then fitted to conform with American regulations and a sparkling new coat of maroon and gold paint was applied.

To accompany the locomotive to the USA, the LMS provided its own crew and mechanics under the supervision of Robert Riddles who had been Stanier's principal assistant and was at that time in charge of the company's motive power affairs in Scotland, while Colonel K. R. N. Speir, the overseas director of the LMS, acted as tour manager. There had been a suggestion that two engine crews would travel over with the locomotive and there was much speculation amongst the LMS footplatemen as to who would be chosen. In the end it was decided that only one crew would be sent and the honour fell to Driver Fred Bishop and Fireman John Carswell of Camden depot. Bishop had joined the old LNWR in 1897 and had progressed to become a top-link driver on Anglo-Scottish expresses. Carswell had been his regular fireman for some time but was also graded as a "passed fireman" and so would be able to take a share in the driving duties if required. The two men leapt to celebrity status over the weeks before their departure and were much in demand for interviews, including one for the television programme *Picture Page* at the Alexandra Palace studio where their "interview" was carefully scripted and rehearsed before the broadcast!

On 9 January 1939 locomotive and train were unveiled to the press at Euston station where they drew much acclaim. One of the main objectives in the design of the train had been to minimise its weight, to

The bell to be carried in the USA is hoisted into position for photographers at Euston. The buckeye coupler and headlamp are already fitted. (The Photo Source/Keystone Press Agency Ltd.)

which end the articulation principle had been adopted and high-tensile steel used in its construction. Great attention was paid to passenger comfort with the provision of oil-filtered ventilation and double windows, while to cut down noise, vibration and draughts much use was made for insulation of cork and asbestos (the deadly hazards of the latter material being yet to be learnt). An innovation in the kitchen was a solid fuel cooking range, developed in conjunction with the British Coal Utilisation Council.

During the display, the locomotives's bell was ceremonially hoisted into position on top of the smokebox after which Bishop and Carswell posed for

Lord Stamp, the LMS Chairman, with Driver Bishop and Fireman Carswell during the "Coronation Scot" press exhibition at Euston on 9 January 1939. (The Photo Source/Keystone Press Agency Ltd.)

1930s style in the "Coronation Scot" club saloon. (National Railway Museum)

publicity photographs, a role to which they were going to become well-accustomed. Due to loading gauge limitations, the bell could not be carried in Britain and it was therefore removed before the engine left the station to continue its test runs with the carriages.

After a farewell luncheon at the Euston Hotel presided over by Lord Stamp, the LMS Chairman, the locomotive and coaches were hauled to Southampton on 19 January and loaded on board the *Belpamela,* an Oslo-registered vessel of a type fitted with permanent railway tracks in the holds. The ship sailed on 26 January and, after a stormy passage, reached Baltimore on 20 February, six days late. Bishop and Carswell followed later aboard the *Aquitania* to New York, while Riddles made the crossing in style on the *Queen Mary.* Both liners reached America ahead of the *Belpamela* and so the LMS team was able to travel to Baltimore to witness the unloading of the train at Locust Point. This took place in extreme weather conditions, with the temperature plummeting from 76°F to 26°F over the two days of the operation, but by 24 February the train had been assembled and entered the Baltimore & Ohio Railroad's Mount Clare workshops to be prepared.

To take the train to New York a 3,121-mile tour had been arranged which involved running over the Baltimore & Ohio, Pennsylvania, Big Four, Louisville & Nashville, Alton, Michigan Central, Boston & Albany and New York, New Haven and Hartford Railroads. The tour began on 21 March, passing through 15 states and visiting 38 towns and cities during its course. The itinerary was as follows:

March		April	
21	Baltimore (Md.)	3	Battle Creek (Mich.)
22	Washington (D.C.)	4	Detroit (Mich.)
23	Wilmington (Del.)	5	Toledo (Ohio)
23	Philadelphia (Pa.)	6	Cleveland (Ohio)
24	Lancaster (Pa.)	6	Akron (Ohio)
25	Harrisburg (Pa.)	7	Youngstown(Ohio)
25	Pittsburgh (Pa.)	7	Erie (Pa.)
26	Wheeling (W.Va.)	8	Buffalo (NY)
27	Columbus (Ohio)	9	Rochester (NY)
27	Dayton (Ohio)	9	Syracuse (NY)
28	Cincinatti (Ohio)	10	Utica (NY)
29	Louisville (Ky.)	10	Schenectady (NY)
30	Indianapolis (Ind.)	11	Albany (NY)
30	Terre Haute (Ind.)	11	Springfield (Mass.)
31	St. Louis (Mo.)	12	Worcester (Mass.)
		13	Boston (Mass.)
April		13	Providence (RI)
1	Springfield (Ill.)	14	Hartford (Conn.)
2	Chicago (Ill.)	14	New Haven (Conn.)
3	Kalamazoo (Mich.)	14	New York City

A good deal of preliminary planning had gone into ensuring the success of the tour. A full stock of tools and equipment - including two spare brick arches for the firebox and six spare firing shovels - was sent out in crates to accompany the "Duchess". A specification had also been supplied for the type of fuel required and as coal from the Kanawa Pocohontas field seemed to be most suitable, stocks were ordered to be available at various locations. For their part, the Americans proved to be the most enthusiastic of hosts, accommodating Riddles and the engine crew in first class hotels and putting a car at their disposal at each overnight stop.

The programme actually commenced on 18 March with a series of press runs between Baltimore and Washington during which several stops were made for the "Coronation Scot" to be photographed alongside crack American expresses. The tour itself attracted tremendous attention and those in charge were taken aback by the queues waiting to see it. At each town, Riddles would change from his overalls in the sleeping car and then call on the Mayor to invite him to open the exhibition. There were 16,000 visitors on the first day of the Baltimore exhibition, 20,000 at St. Louis, 27,000 at Cincinatti and 25,00 at Chicago. At Wilmington the opening had to be brought forward half an hour while at Syracuse so large was the crowd that the train was an hour late departing. By the time New York was reached, around 425,000 people had passed through it.

Many complimentary press reports were received on the quality of both the design and the riding of the locomotive and carriages. In the *Detroit News* a columnist by the name of Esther Beck McIntyre described it as a "a cunning little item. . . . Britain's newest and ritziest train" while the *Syracuse Journal* fastened somewhat scornfully on the engine's "oddly cissy little whistle, more like a child's penny tooter than a great powerful iron horse". But one of the best of a host of favourable reports was compiled by Philip Hampson who travelled from Chicago to St. Louis representing the *Chicago Tribune*:

"After the starting whistle blows the train starts smoothly, so smoothly that motion is hardly perceptible. The passenger looks about and finds himself in toy-sized surroundings. British trains, according to G. D. Collas of the British party, can't be built larger because they must clear existing bridges and tunnels.

"To conserve space the corridors are narrow. Compartments off the corridor have rubber foam seats; comfortable, but not more so than those of American trains. Compartment walls are finished in British Empire wood, with markers telling the varieties. Among them are figured teak from Burma and white sycamore from England. In a recess under the window of each compartment is a telephone with which the steward may be called for food or drinks.

"Generous window space gives good vision. Also, the interior walls of the compartments are glass and the passenger can see out the side opposite the window. This train is air-conditioned, but the windows are not sealed tight. A passenger asked why it was necessary to have windows opening.

" 'If we built a train with windows that wouldn't open', Collas said 'we'd have a revolution. An Englishman will always insist on his right to open a train window'.

"A stroll through the corridor, finished in wood, failed to disclose any ice water container. Almost every American passenger car has one. Collas explained that nobody in England drinks ice water, that it is 'bad for the stomach'.

"The cocktail lounge (so designated) is America in England; seating arrangements, wall decorations and bar are typical. If the car were a little larger, one might think it belonged on an American train.

"The sleeping car has individual rooms, very small. The traveller in England, because of short distances, spends little time in his berth. Berths are at right angles to the window, contrary to general American practice. . . .

"The 'club saloon', or observation car, is finished in England's dark oak. It has colorful red leather seats and trimming. At one end is an electric fireplace. At the end of this car, the last of the train, is a small compartment for the train crew.

"This Coronation Scot is a splendid train, neat, compact as a watch. . . ."

In the guise of No. 6220, the locomotive performed admirably though there was a little disappointment in the LMS camp that it was not allowed to run at more than 85 mph. American "engineers" accompanied the crew for route guidance and it took the LMS men some time to accustom themselves to the fact that "clear" signals were white rather than green as at home. At Chicago, Riddles was presented with an engraved American chime whistle by the Model Railroad Builders of America; however, this was of such a size that it would have been "out of gauge" on the locomotive back in Britain and so it was eventually employed as the Crewe Works hooter, signalling the times of starting and finishing work! At other stops, the newspapers were humoured with endless publicity "photo-calls"; at Utica, for instance, a team of husky dogs accompanying two Canadian

The "Duchess" about to land on American soil at Locust Point, Baltimore, on 22 February 1939. (The Photo Source/Keystone Press Agency Ltd.)

The "Coronation Scot" departing from Baltimore on a press run to Washington on 18 March 1939. (Associated Press Ltd.)

On show at the Grand Central station, Chicago, on 2 April 1939. (Ralph E. Melching collection)

Contrast in streamliners — Coronation *and the Baltimore & Ohio Railroad 4-6-2 No. 5304 (the "Bullet") on the Thomas Viaduct at Relay, Maryland, on 18 March 1938. (Associated Press Ltd.)*

Robert Riddles (left of the buckeye coupler) receives an engraved chime whistle from the Model Railroad Builders of America at Chicago on 2 April 1939. Next to the "Duchess" is one of the first streamlined diesel-electric locomotives, the General Motors class DP-2 No. 55. (National Railway Museum)

trappers were photographed in front of the engine during a 3,000-mile trek from the Arctic Circle to the World's Fair.

The press were much taken with the LMS footplatemen. Bishop and Carswell evidently enjoyed themselves hugely but found American life difficult to get used to and were always ready to pass on their impressions to reporters. Both expressed a preference for pints of ale over the Martinis and cocktails they were offered, while American breakfasts were soon found wanting. "An Englishman eats two rashers of bacon for breakfast that'll take up the 'ole plate", commented Bishop to the *Baltimore Evening Sun.* American tea also came in for heavy criticism, with the crew declaring that "no American knows how to make tea anyway!"

The tour was a triumphant progress but, not surprisingly, things did not *always* go smoothly. Right at the outset Driver Bishop contracted pneumonia (probably as a result of the exceptional weather in which he had watched the unloading of the train) and was admitted to hospital. Riddles therefore shared the footplate duties with Carswell until Bishop was fit enough to rejoin the team on 9 April. In the event, Carswell was promoted to driver while Riddles himself acted as fireman and the press were much intrigued by the sight of an LMS company "executive" shovelling coal.

Trouble was also encountered with the quality of the coal and with the brick arch which began to collapse into the firebox after only three days of the tour. At Harrisburg a spare arch was fitted by the Pennsylvania Railroad but the work was badly done

and a third one had to be put in at St. Louis where, even after allowing the locomotive to cool down, Riddles, his chief mechanic and a local boilersmith were obliged to work in the firebox with 50 lbs. of steam still in the boiler. At Washington six boys were put on probation and ordered to pay costs after pleading guilty to scratching their names on the engine and carriages while on another occasion, en route from St. Louis to Springfield, an emergency stop had to be made to avoid hitting a car whose driver had lost his way and become stuck on the tracks.

On arrival at New York, a reception for 1,000 guests was held on the train which was then handed over to the World's Fair authorities at the Long Island station. The train was on exhibition at the World's Fair site at Flushing Meadow from 30 April to 30 October during which time it was inspected by over two million people. Amongst the other exhibits with which it kept company were an Italian State Railways electric train and the colossal "S-1" 6-4-4-6 of the Pennsylvania Railroad; so it was that the most powerful express locomotive design in Britain could be seen with the most powerful express locomotive in the world.

In his address in the LMS brochure for the World's Fair, Lord Stamp set down his hope that "this new tour of an LMS train will coincide with a new period of peace and prosperity for both our nations". It was not, alas, to be for the triumph of the venture was overshadowed by the political events of the summer in Europe which culminated in Britain's declaration of war with Germany on 3 September. After the Fair closed, the LMS decided not to risk shipping the engine and carriages back to this country and so they returned to Baltimore for storage. The train emerged again to be shown at the 1940 World's Fair where it was viewed by another 1,870,000 visitors before returning once more to Baltimore. There it languished in the Mount Clare workshops, its wheels chained to the rails on the orders of the US customs to prevent any use for revenue-purposes. Various ideas were put forward for making use of the "Coronation Scot" during its enforced exile, including a programme of special trains with traditional British food between New York and Albany during the tourist season or even between New York and Montreal in conjunction with the Delaware & Hudson Railroad. None of these plans came to fruition but at least it fared better than the Italian electric train which was seized for scrap by the federal alien property custodian.

By the end of 1941, however, the need for every available unit of motive power was such that the LMS finally resolved to bring the locomotive home and, after a tense crossing in an Atlantic convoy, it arrived at the Queen Alexandra Dock in Cardiff on 16 February 1942 on board the SS *Pacific Pioneer*. The coaches, meanwhile, were presented to the US Army for use by officers of the Quartermaster Corps at Jeffersonville, Indiana. They were not to return to Britain until after the war but by then the "Coronation Scot" service had disappeared for ever and its vehicles were left to find what work they could on various residential and cruise trains in the North West and North Wales.

Back on the West Coast Main Line

From Cardiff the "Duchess" was hauled to Crewe where, after attention in the Works and the removal of its remaining American fittings, it was put back into traffic on 18 March 1942 in the arduous conditions which prevailed during the war. The bell which the engine had still proudly carried on top of the smokebox when it was unloaded at Cardiff was removed before the journey to Crewe and was later hung in the Works offices. In March 1943 the locomotive again entered Crewe Works for overhaul and as the original 6220 *Coronation* was also there for repair the opportunity was taken to restore to both engines their correct names and numbers. Outshopped on 20 April and now rightfully identified once more as *Duchess of Hamilton,* 6229 managed to retain its maroon livery even though other members of the class were being turned out in plain black but wartime austerity eventually caught up with it and by 1945 it too found itself clad in this drab fashion.

In 1945 the LMS decided to remove the casing from its streamliners to simplify servicing and maintenance. This was done over the next three years as the engines passed through the shops and *Duchess of Hamilton* was the penultimate member of the class to be dealt with. In fact, it completed its LMS days in its original condition, emerging de-streamlined in LMS post-war lined black livery at the start of the nationalised British Railways era in 1948, with smoke

Back home after three years in exile, the "Duchess" awaits unloading at Cardiff on 16 February 1942. (Welsh Industrial & Maritime Museum)

Duchess of Hamilton *in plain black livery at Camden shed in 1946. (S. Teasdale)*

deflectors, double chimney and the sloping smokebox top which for a few years was a distinctive feature of the former streamliners.

In 1950 46229 (as it was now numbered by BR) was given the new blue livery with black and white lining which had been adopted, after a series of experiments, for express locomotives. This livery did not, however, prove very durable in service, being discarded in 1951 in favour of Brunswick green with orange and black lining, based on the GWR style, and *Duchess of Hamilton* was repainted in this colour scheme in April 1953 during a "Heavy Intermediate" overhaul at Crewe.

Following its return from the USA, *Duchess of Hamilton* had alternated its home allegiances between Crewe North and Camden depots but in July 1952 it began an allocation to Camden which was to endure for the next eight years. During the 1950s the railway system maintained the process of recovery from the ravages of war and the "Coronation" Pacifics were able to continue to demonstrate their supremacy on the West Coast Main Line. They were in charge of the principal expresses between Euston and Glasgow (including such distinguished named trains as the "Royal Scot" and the "Mid-Day Scot") as well as the heaviest trains between Liverpool and the capital. They also worked from time to time over the North Wales coast line to Holyhead and to Manchester via Crewe (they were prohibited from the Stoke route) while in Scotland they ventured north as far as Perth and appeared on the former Glasgow & South Western route via Dumfries and Kilmarnock.

Amongst the most prestigious railway workings are those of the Royal Train and journeys over the West Coast Main Line were frequently entrusted to the "Coronations", especially if the heavy overnight train was involved. One such occasion on which *Duchess of Hamilton* was employed on Royal Train duty occurred on 17 May 1956 when members of the Royal Family travelled from Euston to Ballater for a holiday at Balmoral. 46229 hauled the train (conveying the Queen, Prince Charles and Princess Anne) as far as Carlisle, reached non-stop after leaving Euston at 7.00 pm. Meticulous planning had, as always, gone into its running and detailed instructions were issued to staff to ensure its smooth operation, even down to an order that a supply of evening newspapers, two copies of the *Radio Times* and the latest issue of *Sporting Life* were to be put on board at Euston!

In January 1957 46229 entered Crewe Works for another "Heavy Intermediate" overhaul, re-entering traffic on 2 March with a standard round-topped smokebox. Later that year came the surprising decision by the London Midland Region to repaint some of its Pacifics in a maroon livery akin to that of the LMS and 46229 was one of sixteen "Coronations" to be so adorned, being turned out in this colour scheme in September 1958 after another repair at Crewe. At first the lining on the cab and tender was of the BR fashion set in from the edges but the more familiar LMS-style lining around the edges of the panels was subsequently applied.

In 1955 British Railways had published its Modernisation Plan which portended the eventual demise of steam in favour of diesel and electric traction. At the time, though, such a transition was expected to take fifteen to twenty years to achieve — and steam still had a few more fine hours to come. In 1957 BR decided to introduce a new high-speed service between Euston and Glasgow which was to be

Duchess of Hamilton *at the start of the British Railways era in 1948, de-streamlined and in a rather hybrid livery — LMS lined black but with its BR number, 46229. (National Railway Museum)*

46229 pulls away from Carlisle at the head of a London express in the mid-50s. (Eric Treacy/Millbrook House collection)

Duchess of Hamilton *in BR green at Willesden depot in 1957. (J. P. Mullet/Colour Rail)*

46229 in its early form of maroon livery, with BR-style lining, passing Rugby No. 1 box with the down "Royal Scot" in May 1959. (D. Smith/Colour Rail)

Permanent way work in progress at Dudswell as 46229 passes cautiously with a down express in June 1961. (J. P. Mullett/Colour Rail)

46229 on Royal Train duty. Several of the vehicles have also joined the engine in the National Collection.

Duchess of Hamilton *departs from Carlisle station, bound for London with the ''Royal Scot'' in 1956. (F. W. Shuttleworth)*

Duchess of Hamilton *backs its stock out of Euston after arriving with the inaugural up ''Caledonian'' on 17 June 1957. (Martin Welch)*

With main line passenger work running out for the "Coronations", 46229 is found on express parcels duty approaching Chester from North Wales towards the end of its BR career. (J. R. Carter)

a limited load flyer with 84 First Class and 120 Second Class seats operating on a 6 hr 40 min schedule in both directions. The new service — named "The Caledonian" — commenced on 17 June 1957 and *Duchess of Hamilton* was rostered for the inaugural southbound train, reaching London two minutes early. 46229 was again in the news on 7 August when, working the up "Caledonian", it reached London in 6 hr. 27 min. from Glasgow, averaging 74.1 mph between Crewe and Euston, a run widely reported in the press and on the radio.

In October 1960 46229 was transferred back to Crewe North depot, moving on the following March to Liverpool's Edge Hill shed where it was to be based for the remainder of its BR career. By the early 60s it had become evident that the end of steam was going to come a lot sooner than orginally envisaged. On the West Coast Main Line, the new Type 4 (Class 40) diesel-electric locomotives were displacing the "Coronations" from the prime express duties - though they were regularly required to stand in for failures - and the mighty Pacifics often came to be seen on relatively humble activities.

For instance, on 31 August 1962 *Duchess of Hamilton* was employed on the season's penultimate "Lakes Express" which it hauled from Crewe as far as Penrith by which time the load was a mere five coaches for Keswick and Workington. From 8 October until 2 February 1963 it languished in store but during the

spring and summer of 1963 the engine was kept occupied in one way or another. In March it had a spell on loan back to Camden while later in the summer it shared with other Edge Hill Pacifics haulage of the 7.00 pm express freight from Pocket Nook goods yard, St. Helens, to Carlisle and Glasgow. On 14 July 46229 was reported off its beaten track at Newton Heath shed in Manchester and the next day worked the 9.30 am Manchester (Victoria)-Glasgow express, relieving a Type 4 diesel-electric which had failed at Bolton, while on 27 July it was found at the head of a Crewe-Glasgow parcels train waiting impatiently in the loop at Penrith as a succession of expresses overtook it on the main line.

Duchess of Hamilton was put into store again on 14 October but emerged for a spell of work over the busy Christmas period. On 17 December it was back on express passenger duty, hauling the up Heysham-Euston "Ulster Express" and two days later it was spotted at Preston, without its nameplates, on an early morning special parcels working from Carlisle to Wigan. These, however, were to be the last calls upon its services for suitable work for the "Coronations" was running out. The first members of the class had been withdrawn at the end of 1962 and within two years they had all gone. On 30 December 1963 46229 returned to store and on 15 February 1964 it was officially withdrawn from traffic, having covered for the LMS and BR a total of 1,533,846 miles.

The electrification catenary provides a portent of things to come as 46229 heads out of Liverpool past West Allerton in the summer of 1961. (J. A. Roxburgh)

46229 backs onto the turntable at Holyhead depot during the summer of 1962. (Tudor Jones)

A work-stained Duchess of Hamilton *after arrival at Euston with the 9.43 am from Wolverhampton on 11 March 1963, (John Edgington)*

...and so to the National Railway Museum

In 1961 the British Transport Commission had published a list of locomotives considered appropriate for official preservation, as a result of which an example of the "Coronation" class — No. 46235 *City of Birmingham* — was set aside and presented to the city of its name to be exhibited in the Birmingham Museum of Science & Industry. The withdrawal of the class, however, took place before the spread of the great steam preservation movement in the mid-60s and the rest of the "Coronations" might all have been shunted into the scrapyards had it not been for a decision from a somewhat unlikely quarter.

Butlins Ltd. wished to acquire some large locomotives as attractions at certain of its holiday camps and by the summer of 1963 had installed No. 6100 *Royal Scot* at Skegness and No. 6203 *Princess Margaret Rose* at Pwllheli. Early in 1964 two "Coronations" were purchased — *Duchess of Sutherland* and *Duchess of Hamilton* for display at Heads of Ayr and Minehead respectively. Accordingly, *Duchess of Hamilton* was turned out of Crewe Works in April after external refurbishment as LMS No. 6229 and was hauled to its new home in Somerset. For its new owners the engine had been painted in a form of maroon livery which, though impressive, was historically inaccurate — in LMS days it had only carried this colour as a streamliner.

Duchess of Hamilton was on show at the Minehead camp by the start of the 1964 season and there it stood for the next ten years, a source of wonder to the mildly curious. Not surprisingly, the exposed conditions only ¼-mile from the sea gradually took their toll and as early as August 1968 a correspondent in the *Railway Magazine* was commenting on the locomotive's deterioration. But rescue was still some time away.

In 1970 Butlins resolved to find new custodians for its engines and the following year *Duchess of Sutherland* and *Royal Scot* took up residence at the Bressingham Steam Museum in Norfolk. In 1971 the Transport Trust was asked to help place the remaining locomotives and, with 6229's condition continuing to cause concern, it was plain that action would have to be taken before long. The cost and physical difficulty of moving it were proving considerable deterrents, however, but in 1974 the prospects for 6229 at last began to look brighter.

In York the new National Railway Museum was being set up and a suggestion was made to its parent body, the Science Museum, that *Duchess of Hamilton* might be a fitting exhibit. By February 1975 negotiations had been successfully concluded with Butlins for the locomotive to be placed on a 20-year loan to the NRM and arrangements were put in hand for it to be transported by rail to Swindon Works for restoration to exhibition standard.

This itself was a major operation. The branch from Taunton to Minehead had by then been closed for five years but a trial run by a BR diesel locomotive found it intact. This was fortunate as weight restrictions on the roads in the area had meant that, if the engine could not travel by rail, the only other option would have been to dismantle it where it stood and the cost of such an exercise might have proved prohibitive. Next came the preparation of the locomotive for movement after a decade of inactivity but, despite its open-air situation, the "Duchess" had been well cared for, with all its moving parts protected by grease and silver paint. The task of preparing it was given to the Dart Valley Railway, a task which mainly consisted of ensuring plenty of lubrication to the axleboxes, motion and cylinders. On 10 March 1975 *Duchess of Hamilton* at last departed the holiday camp to be conveyed by low-loader to Minehead station, its tender following the next day. On 13 March it was hauled gingerly over the branch to Taunton, stopping regularly to check for hot boxes, and three days later it arrived at Swindon. It had been a difficult operation which had owed much to the goodwill of the British Railways Board, the Western Region and the Works Manager at Swindon.

There had been a good deal of discussion on the extent of the restoration to be undertaken at Swindon, with both the re-application of streamlining and a return to working order being considered and rejected as too expensive. In the end, it was decided that the locomotive should be displayed in the condition in which it last ran in service — in BR maroon livery as No. 46229. Even cosmetic restoration, involving the renewal of much platework and boiler cladding and the manufacture of new smoke deflectors, occupied fully twelve months and cost over £17,000.

On 20/21 May 1976 *Duchess of Hamilton* was hauled to York via Gloucester, Stratford-upon-Avon, Birmingham and Derby and on 26 May it was formally unveiled in the National Railway Museum at a dinner to commemorate the centenary of the birth of its designer, William Stanier. For the next two years the locomotive rested in splendour inside the Museum, during which time it became the subject of much speculation by enthusiasts on the possibility of it steaming again. But with the NRM's responsibility extending only to maintaining the engine in exhibition condition and with countless other demands on its resources, no funds could be spared for such a project. Nevertheless, events were still moving in 46229's favour.

Firstly, the founding in 1977 of a supporting body — the Friends of the National Railway Museum — paved the way for externally-raised money to be used to assist the Museum in specific ventures. Secondly, one of the NRM's senior curatorial officers was David Jenkinson, an ardent advocate of the LMS in general and the "Coronations" in particular. Towards the end of 1976 he was able to interest the fine-art printers Manuscript in a scheme to return *Duchess of Hamilton*

On its first outing after returning to steam, Duchess of Hamilton *near Micklefield with the ''Limited Edition'' on 10 May 1980. (R. Jones/Colour Rail)*

An LMS Pacific on the East Coast Main Line! 46229 approaching York at Skelton Jn. on 10 May 1980, a scene now transformed by electrification. (Hugh Ballantyne)

Duchess of Hamilton *as repainted for Butlins Ltd. at Crewe in April 1964 prior to leaving for Minehead holiday camp.*

A forlorn sight at Minehead camp in February 1974. Behind the engine's tender is LBSCR "Terrier" 0-6-0T Knowle. *(J. A. Coiley)*

The "Duchess" is eased gently over the Minehead-Taunton branch on 13 March 1975, passing Blue Anchor en route to Swindon and, later, the National Railway Museum. (R. O. Coffin)

One of Duchess of Hamilton's *first assignments after its return to steam in 1980 was a special marking the 150th anniversary of the Liverpool & Manchester Railway. It is seen here at Sheffield Midland en route from York to Manchester on 13 September prior to working the train the next day. (L. A. Nixon)*

to working order. This would be achieved by the sale of a limited edition print from a specially-commissioned painting by the celebrated artist Terence Cuneo showing the locomotive climbing Beattock bank, with a proportion of the revenue being channelled into a fund administered by the Friends. It was the first enterprise of its kind to assist a single piece of railway restoration.

So it was that in May 1978 46229 was taken out of the Museum, first of all for Cuneo to sketch it for his painting and then for the overhaul to begin. Whilst financial support was assured, there nevertheless remained substantial technical problems to be solved. Although inspection had found that the boiler and firebox were in good condition, all the small tubes needed replacement but the large tubes and all but two superheater elements were sounder than expected and were able to be retained. However, the main steam pipe from the regulator to the superheater header had collapsed and considerable ingenuity had to be exercised in fitting a replacement without the additional expense of removing some or all of the flue tubes. Subsequently, a hairline crack in the superheater header caused more anxiety and the tender water space was found to contain paper-thin platework in places. Fortunately a good deal of preliminary work had been done at Swindon, including the removal of the blue asbestos boiler lagging and attention to the running gear, but many other fittings had to be overhauled or replaced. These tribulations upset all the estimates of workload, timescale and expenditure and despite the success of the print sale it became clear that

the money raised would not meet the final cost, so the Friends agreed to contribute the balance from their funds.

At last, on 14 April 1980, 46229 was steamed for the first time since December 1963 and on 1 May made a successful trial run to South Milford and back, attaining 60 mph on the return. The stage was now set for the long-awaited reappearance of a "Coronation" on the main line and in the glorious spring sunshine of 10 May *Duchess of Hamilton* hauled two trains over the York-Leeds-Harrogate-York circle. The inaugural trains were titled "The Limited Edition" and appropriately carried those who, by purchasing the prints or in other ways, had made the whole thing possible.

Later in the month 46229 participated in the cavalcade of locomotives at Rainhill marking the 150th anniversary of the Liverpool & Manchester Railway and in September, on the actual date of the line's opening, hauled a commemorative train between the two cities. At Eccles a stop was made for "VIPs" to be taken behind the veteran L&MR locomotive *Lion* into the original Manchester station at Liverpool Road. In 1938, when the "Duchess" was brand new, it had been photographed at Crewe alongside *Lion* — who could have imagined that over 40 years on the two would meet again, both of them in steam?

Over the next five years *Duchess of Hamilton* became a regular and often outstanding performer on special trains on British Rail tracks, most of which took it over routes that never saw locomotives of this class in normal service. For instance, the autumn of 1980 found the engine in action on the Trans-Pennine route

46229 climbing towards Standedge Tunnel with a Liverpool-York special on 11 November 1980 commemorating 150 years of the carriage of mail on railways. (David Nixon)

Duchess of Hamilton *departs from Scarborough with the inaugural BR "Scarborough Spa Express" on 23 May 1981. (W. A. Sharman)*

With the NRM's Royal Train brake No. 5155 as support coach, 46229 passes the splendid LNWR signal box at Chester after turning on the triangle during a run from York to Crewe on 26 May 1981. (Martin Welch)

Duchess of Hamilton *rounds the curves of the Derwent Valley near Kirkham Abbey with the inaugural "Scarborough Spa Express" on 23 May 1981.*
(Chris Hogg/National Railway Museum)

An unprecedented setting for a "Coronation" Pacific — Parton, between Workington and Whitehaven, on the Cumbrian Coast line on 11 August 1982. (David Chambers)

A traditional shed scene for the "Duchess" at Carnforth on 12 April 1982. In front of the coaling tower is Lancashire & Yorkshire Railway 0-6-0 No. 1300. (W. A. Sharman)

between Manchester and Leeds through Standedge Tunnel and making an eagerly-anticipated debut on the Settle-Carlisle line. Circumstances conspired to render it a disappointing first run — but better things were to come.

The following year 46229 made two visits to Scarborough, firstly to test the newly-reinstated turntable at the resort and then to launch BR's "Scarborough Spa Express" service. The engine also made a return to its "birthplace" at Crewe Works, reached via the Cheshire Lines route and Chester, receiving mechanical attention to the front bogie, the foundation ring and a cracked driving wheel spoke before starring at a Works open day. A much more confident return was made to the Settle-Carlisle line during 1981, with 46229 giving a foretaste of its potential on this demanding route.

In 1982 a series of visits was made to Carnforth, with *Duchess of Hamilton* staying at the Steamtown Railway Museum alongside its old stamping ground on the West Coast Main Line. The "Long Drag" was tackled again and amongst the more unusual routes travelled by the "Duchess" was the Cumbrian Coast line from Carlisle to Carnforth via Workington, while in the autumn the locomotive headed to the Welsh Borders to haul a programme of excursions between Chester, Hereford and Newport.

1983 began with some quite outstanding performances on the Settle-Carlisle route. However, not all 46229's duties are of such a strenuous nature and one of its more singular engagements came in June when the locomotive was given a cameo role in the film *The Dresser* which had the distinction of being presented at the 1984 Royal Film Première. "Made up" as LMS No. 6229, the "Duchess" performed impeccably in front of the cameras with a cast which included such names as Albert Finney and Tom Courtenay. A welcome return to Scotland was made in October 1983 when 46229 traversed the former Glasgow & South Western route to Ayr to attend a BR open day at the depot and the year concluded with another special train over the Settle-Carlisle line, this time arranged by local authorities in support of the campaign to resist its proposed closure. During this, a press conference was held at Garsdale in front of the locomotive, with representatives of various councils, tourist boards and BR holding forth in spite of being enshrouded in drizzle, low cloud and steam!

In August 1983, however, there took place the only untoward incident to befall *Duchess of Hamilton* since its return to service when, hauling the return "Scarborough Spa Express", a blowback from the firebox occurred inside Bramhope Tunnel between Leeds and Harrogate. An emergency brake application was made and regrettably the driver sustained burns to his arm. Locomotive and crew were able to complete the journey back to York where examination of the smokebox revealed the loss of a core plug from the blower casting which had caused a loss of vacuum and the release of steam at boiler pressure into the smokebox. An inquiry was held which recommended new procedures for the removal and renewal of these plugs at intervals of not less than ten years and the episode served as a timely reminder (if one were needed) that the operation of steam locomotives, however much it may be for pleasure, is never a business to be undertaken lightly.

1984 will be remembered for the prolonged period of hot, dry weather which prevailed from early April right through the summer. These conditions posed exceptional problems for locomotive operators and a crop of lineside blazes brought forth an edict that engines be fitted with spark-arresting devices in the smokebox. 46229's activities were mainly confined to the familiar Carlisle and Scarborough itineraries but there *were* one or two unusual assignments. In June, during a week's stay in Carlisle, the engine was booked for two Appleby-Edinburgh excursions organised by BR for local schoolchildren. *Duchess of Hamilton* worked the trains as far as Carlisle, stopping to pick up passengers at Langwathby, Lazonby and Armathwaite — undoubtedly the first time an LMS Pacific had called at these village stations! A month later, the locomotive was chartered by BR's Railfreight sector for a special train from Huddersfield to York and back for the Butterley Building Co. with which a lucrative contract had just been signed but on the return journey the "Duchess" started an embankment fire near Church Fenton, resulting in it being diesel-hauled home to York in disgrace!

Duchess of Hamilton crosses *Eskmeals Viaduct after leaving Ravenglass with the "Cumbrian Coast Express" on 11 August 1982. (W. A. Sharman)*

1985, by contrast, was a year of considerable adventure. 46229 began by blazing a new trail for the class in the North East, covering the East Coast Main Line between York and Newcastle, the coastal route to Newcastle via Sunderland and the Newcastle-Carlisle line. This was followed at Easter by another "first", a run to Scarborough via Hull and Bridlington. But the main event of the year was to be an exhibition at Swindon Works to celebrate the 150th anniversary of the founding of the Great Western Railway to which *Duchess of Hamilton* had been invited to fly the flag for the LMS. Accordingly, 46229 headed south in May — to London, in fact, reached via Sheffield, Toton, Birmingham, Banbury and over former Great Central metals into Marylebone station. This was its first visit to the capital since 1963 and, during a scheduled two-month stay before proceeding to Swindon, 46229 made several appearances on a new and successful itinerary to Stratford-upon-Avon over a route which offered the engine ample opportunity to show its capacity for hill climbing and fast running. A week was also spent on display at Aylesbury, with the locomotive traversing the single track branch from Princes Risborough.

However, the Swindon exhibition was cancelled in the wake of the repurcussions which followed the untimely announcement that the Works was to close and so *Duchess of Hamilton* remained at Marylebone throughout the summer, adding to its growing reputation on the Stratford route. 46229 *did* manage to attend a GWR 150 event in the end — an open day at Old Oak Common depot in September where two other National Collection locomotives, *King George V* and the broad gauge replica *Iron Duke*, were among the various star turns.

The five months that *Duchess of Hamilton* spent in London was the longest period it had been away from York and operating a locomotive some 200 miles from its home base is a demanding commitment, especially if things go wrong. Such a problem arose on 29 June when a portion of the brick arch collapsed into the firebox on leaving Stratford and with another trip arranged for the next day there was no alternative but for the "Duchess" to carry on. A new arch subsequently had to be put in but even before that 46229's London season had almost been cut short when the engine's cab roof was discovered to be fouling the underside of a bridge at Willesden Green. Fortunately it was the height of the track that was found to be at fault and, after attention to the ballast to correct the gauge, the "Duchess" was able to resume its programme.

Throughout 1985 all concerned with the locomotive had been aware that 46229's boiler certificate expired at the end of October, a fact which would conclude this particular chapter in its story. Early in October the "Duchess" returned to York on a memorable run from Marylebone and on 19 and 26 October made its farewell appearances before being withdrawn from service. Appropriately, these were over the Settle-Carlisle line on which it had set new standards in locomotive performance and *Duchess of Hamilton* bowed out in style, with two more stirring ascents of the Pennine hills. Since its return to steam in 1980 the "Duchess" had completed 13,223 miles (without a single mechanical failure whilst out on the main line), making a total of 1,547,069 miles since entering traffic in 1938.

The smoke deflectors fitted to the ''Coronations'' were not always as effective as intended at preventing exhaust drifting down the smokebox, as shown by this view of 46229 passing the now-closed and demolished Peckfield Colliery between York and Leeds on 20 February 1982. Behind the locomotive are the NRM's 1960 Pullman cars Eagle *and* Emerald *providing a full meal service on a ''55 Club'' operation. (L. A. Nixon)*

Maryport station, once headquarters of the Maryport & Carlisle Railway, is the unlikely setting for 46229 on 11 August 1982. (W. A. Sharman)

A "Duchess" on the Cumbrian Coast route — 46229 follows the bleak coastline at Nethertown on 11 August 1982. (W. A. Sharman)

Duchess of Hamilton *makes a stirring ascent of Gresford bank with the "Welsh Marches Pullman" to Shrewsbury on 23 October 1982. (Ken Bull)*

Duchess of Hamilton *passing Marsden, climbing towards Standedge Tunnel, en route from York to Chester and Shrewsbury with the NRM Pullman cars on 23 October 1982.*
(Hugh Ballantyne)

A water stop from a road tanker on an overbridge at Kirkconnel during 46229's return journey from Ayr to Carlisle over the Glasgow & South Western line on 31 October 1983.
(David Chambers)

A north eastern snowscape is the setting for 46229 as it passes Gateshead alongside the Tyne & Wear Metro on 16 March 1985. (L. A. Nixon)

The station clock records the time as 11.36 as 46229 runs past Great Western lower-quadrant signals into Banbury on 30 June 1985. (Keith Jackson)

Duchess of Hamilton *passes a London Transport train on the Central Line as it heads out of the capital at Brondesbury with a ''Sunday Lunch'' excursion to Stratford-upon-Avon on 12 May 1985. (W. A. Sharman)*

The ''Duchess'' storms out of Blea Moor Tunnel with the northbound ''Cumbrian Mountain Express'' on 29 October 1983. (Paul Stephens)

46229 hard at work amidst wild Pennine moorland, nearing the end of the climb towards Ais Gill summit on 29 October 1983. (Paul Stephens)

A ''Duchess'' on Tyneside — 46229 brings the ''Northern Belle'' across the King Edward Bridge at Newcastle on 16 March 1985. (Peter Such)

Passing Washwood Heath yard, Duchess of Hamilton *makes a fast departure from Birmingham on 5 October 1985. (W. A. Sharman)*

A Suitable Case for Treatment

Over the years between 1980 and 1985 *Duchess of Hamilton* established a reputation second to none for reliability and the quality of its main line performances and since 1981 the funding of the locomotive's operations has been met by the Friends of the NRM. The basis for the continuing programme of maintenance and the overhaul due after 1985 was built up by revenue set aside from earnings from special trains along with ancilliary fund-raising activities such as souvenir sales.

A good deal of work was carried out on the engine after its return to steam to keep it in first-class order and, indeed, improve its performance. During the spring and summer of 1982 the brake and carriage warming systems and the safety valves were overhauled and the regulator valve refaced. Major work was done by Riley & Sons Ltd., mill engineers of Heywood in Lancashire, who rebored the valve liners and fitted new piston valve rings. They also fitted new piston valve heads and rings, remetalled the piston crosshead slide blocks and reconditioned the slide bars. New piston rings were fitted and these repairs had a noticeably improving effect on the locomotive's water consumption. New ball joint ends were fitted to the superheater elements in May 1984 while in September the exhaust injector was overhauled through the good offices of Davies & Metcalfe Ltd., the original manufacturers. Sister locomotive *Duchess of Sutherland* also helped to keep 46229 on the road, with the Bressingham Steam Museum providing on loan a replacement blastpipe and bogie spring from 6233 while repairs to the originals were carried out.

However, the expiry of the boiler certificate in October 1985 meant that all the boiler tubes would have to be removed to permit a full internal inspection of the boiler prior to retubing. Lifting of the boiler from the frames was also necessary to enable examination of the firebox foundation ring and to enable the ashpan to be renewed. Much other work was required as well but fortunately the National Railway Museum saw 46229 as its "flagship" locomotive and so gave approval for the Friends to embark on financing what was, in effect, the equivalent of a Heavy General Repair in a Works.

A "shopping list" of work known to be necessary had been drawn up in readiness for the engine's withdrawal. Apart from the boiler work, this included remetalling of the coupled axleboxes, machining of the wheel bosses, renewal of rivets in the main frames and the overhaul of the trailing truck, brake gear and pipework. The bearing springs had to be reconditioned and the spring hanger gear overhauled, the brake cylinders of both locomotive and tender were to be rebored and the piston rings renewed, while the smokebox door and sections of the footplating required replacement. On the tender, repairs were needed to the tank platework and to the frames and frame stays.

Early in 1986 removal of the tubes began and problems soon began to present themselves, starting with the smokebox which proved to be wasted enough to call for complete renewal. More seriously, inspection of the copper firebox revealed cracks in the doorplate flanges and defects in both tubeplates which were going to need specialist attention. Accordingly, a contract was awarded to C. H. Thompson Ltd. of Oldham to undertake all the necessary boiler and firebox repairs, including retubing and the fitting of a new smokebox, at their own premises.

The firebox of the "Duchess" is made of ⅝″ thick copper, with the plates flanged and formed to produce the required shape, and when cracking occurs it is usually at the rivetted joints. Copper is a difficult metal to weld and, as the first attempts at repairs using conventional methods were unsuccessful, approaches were made to the British Oxygen Co. for expert advice. At length a method of repairing the cracks was recommended which involved pre-heating the entire firebox for three hours to ensure even expansion, a course of action which took four men with no less than fifteen cylinders of oxygen and five of propane. The area around each crack was then heated to 400-500°C before repairing it with a small weld about 2″ long, following which the heating was maintained for a further hour to allow the box to cool slowly and evenly. Welding repairs were also carried out to the copper tubeplate and the steel tubeplate radius and after the copper tubeplate holes had been ferruled the boiler was ready for retubing. Finally came the fitting of the new smokebox and door and the boiler could be reunited with the rest of the locomotive, an operation carried out on 7 March 1989.

The condition of the tender tank gave much cause for concern when stripping of the old paint revealed platework completely wasted through in places and evidence of previous patching of thin metal. There would clearly have to be a considerable amount of platework renewal and the prospect of this major surgery gave rise to thoughts of putting the internal layout of the tender to more advantageous use. Plans were therefore drawn up to raise the water capacity to 5,000 gallons (an increase of 1,000 gallons) while reducing the coal capacity to 8 tons (a loss of 2 tons). The benefits of carrying extra water on the modern railway system, where servicing facilities are not readily available, are obvious whilst the engine's coal capacity has never proved critical. Eventually, however, it was decided that a completely new tender tank should be fabricated to the new design, enabling the original to be retained unaltered for cosmetic restoration for the time when 46229's activities ultimately cease.

The start of the long road back — 46229's boiler being lifted from the frames on 6 May 1986 to be sent away for repair by specialist contractors. (Chris Hogg/National Railway Museum)

In the midst of all this upheaval came the decision by Butlins to sell 46229, along with the other locomotives which had been loaned to various bodies. The terms of the agreement between the NRM and Butlins provided for the Museum to have first option on its purchase and negotiations during 1987 resulted in the formal acquisition of *Duchess of Hamilton* for the National Collection, so securing its future in the most appropriate way possible.

By the end of 1989 work on the "Duchess" was sufficiently advanced for the locomotive to be put into steam on 9 December for the first time for over four years for the benefit of some of those who had contributed to the overhaul appeal fund and five days later a full steam test was carried out to the satisfaction of BR's boiler inspector, enabling a new boiler certificate to be issued.

So what does the future hold for *Duchess of Hamilton*? The comprehensive overhaul undertaken between 1986 and 1990 — one of the most thorough ever — should ensure the continued operation of 46229 for as long as steam is able to run on BR tracks. Who can say whither the engine will travel and what it will achieve in the coming years for so much has happened in the world of main line steam preservation that could not have been envisaged when BR abandoned steam in 1968 and enforced a ban on the running of privately-owned locomotives. The presence of the "Duchess" on the main lines added a new dimension to steam performance in the 1980s, a view which will surely be shared by all who have thrilled to see, hear and travel behind this most charismatic of locomotives. We hope that many more will, in the future, come to see and ride behind *Duchess of Hamilton* on one of its main line outings or to admire it standing in splendour in its home at the National Railway Museum and reflect that *this* really *was* express steam power at its finest. The first fifty years have been interesting enough — here's to the next!

The "Duchess" passing Wilmcote on the climb out of Stratford-upon-Avon with a return "Sunday Lunch" special to London on 12 May 1985. (J. A. Roxburgh)

Sherriff Brow Viaduct is the setting for Duchess of Hamilton *on 19 October 1985 on its last northbound run over the Settle-Carlisle line before being taken out of service. (Paul Stephens)*

PERFORMANCE

Following No. 6220 *Coronation's* 114 mph on the demonstration run of 29 June 1937, the ''Coronations'' settled down to regular service well within their capacity. It was only on the testing of No. 6234 *Duchess of Abercorn* in 1939 with both single and double chimneys that the power potential of these machines was made apparent. With a trailing load of 610 tons made up of 20 bogie coaches, No. 6234 achieved a maximum drawbar horsepower of 2511 equivalent to 2,900 on the level. The LMS calculated the cylinder horsepower at 3,348 indicated horsepower. These were regarded as the highest figures produced by any British steam locomotive — that is until *Duchess of Hamilton* was extended to maximum output and worked at 50% cut-off where *Duchess of Abercorn* had been worked at 30% at the same speed, producing 3,100 equivalent dbhp, at least 3,600 ihp in the cylinders.

The following logs have been collected to show all aspects of the best of ''Coronation'' class working, fortunately all by 46229 in service and they are complemented by examples of some of the best work by this locomotive since preservation and restoration.

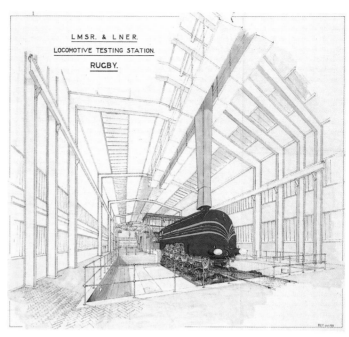

A pre-war architect's impression of the proposed testing plant at Rugby, an LMS/LNER joint venture. The plant was not opened until after the railways had been nationalised in 1948 and the ''Coronations'' de-streamlined. No. 46225 was tested on the rollers of the plant but maximum power outputs were limited, due to fears of wheel-slip and damage to equipment. Road tests carried out on the same machine a year or so later showed certain discrepancies and no comprehensive Bulletin was prepared for general publication (as was the case with a number of other types). (National Railway Museum)

7 January 1984 and 46229 is being worked extremely hard at Mallerstang on the climb to Ais Gill. This was the fastest run up from Appleby and one of the last before a speed restriction was imposed at Kirkby Stephen. Although working a locomotive like this (reminiscent of the old LNWR) is heavy on coal, F.D. Porta of Argentina has shown that such waste can be eliminated by the use of his gas-producer combustion system and high-efficiency draughting. A ''Coronation'' could be worked like this (but without the ''clag'') under service conditions with suitable modifications, including mechanical stoking. (Paul Stephens)

Dist.	Engines, 4-6-2 No. Load (coaches) Load (tons tare) Load (tons gross)	Sched.	46229 16 487 510		46229 16 500 535		"Deltic" 15 451 485	
Miles		min.	m. s.	mph	m. s.	mph	m. s.	mph
0.0	WATFORD	0	0 00	—	0 00	—	0 00	—
3.5	Kings Langley	—	5 56	54½	5 58	57	6 22	51
7.1	Hemel Hempstead	—	9 37	59½	9 34	62		
10.6	Berkhamstead	—	13 04	62	12 52	64	12 38	73
14.3	TRING	16	16 35	63/74	16 20	64/73	15 44	71
			p.w.s.	*55		*47		
18.7	Cheddington	—	20 30	59	20 20		19 16	78/25*
22.8	Leighton	—	24 03	77/81½	24 16	71		
			p.w.s.	*47				
29.3	BLETCHLEY	28	29 28		29 40	74	30 29	77
35.0	Wolverton	—	34 59	70½/74	34 17	78	34 44	85
			p.w.s.	*24				
42.5	ROADE	39	44 01	41	40 45	62	40 22	75/21*
45.4	BLISWORTH	42	47 10	62	43 25	71½		
52.3	Weedon	48	52 59	79½	49 06	73½	52 00	76
57.9	Welton	—	57 20	71½/80½	54 02	64½	56 21	78/80
					p.w.s.	*37		
65.2	RUGBY	60	63 10	*50	62 47	*32	62 12	39*
70.7	Brinklow	—	68 55	65/71½	69 03	64		
			74 53	sig.	pass			
76.1	Bulkington	—	75 55	stop	73 57	70/76		
					p.w.s.	*15		
79.7	NUNEATON	74	81 19	66	78 48	56	75 54	78
84.9	Atherstone	—	85 52	70½	83 58	66		
89.1	Polesworth	—	89 11	79½/82	87 28	76½		
92.6	TAMWORTH	87	91 46	80/82½	90 12	80	86 01	80
98.9	LICHFIELD	93	96 30	75½/74	95 07	68½	91 11	61
103.6	Armitage	—	100 13	81	99 15	73		
106.9	RUGELEY	100	102 40	79	101 53	76½	98 37	67
112.1	Milford	105	106 53	78½	106 10	70		
116.2	STAFFORD	110	110 44	*42/57½	110 01	*54	107 46	*57
			p.w.s.	*30				
121.5	Norton Bridge	116	117 27	40	115 02	66½	113 26	61
126.0	Standon Bridge	—	122 34	60	119 01	71½		
130.3	Whitmore	125	126 33	63	122 36	74½	122 11	58
132.8	Madeley	—	128 55	72½	124 35	79		
135.9	Betley Road	—	131 22	85½	126 54	86	127 14	74
			sigs.	*	sig stop	*	sig stop	
140.7	CREWE	136	138 13	—	136 43	—	136 57	
140.7	Net times (min.)	136	124	—	125¼	—	125¼	

* Service slack

Table 2
Logs of 46229 on heavy down Euston expresses on the WCML and a comparison with "Deltic" on a slightly lighter load. In expert hands, even heavy loads hold no terrors for a "Duchess" in good nick even on tight timings. (See Railway Magazine, C. J. Allen, July 1955; O. S. Nock January 1962).

Table 3 (Above right)
Logs of Duchess of Hamilton on the Northern leg of the "Caledonian". The ability to accelerate the lighter train away from out of course checks even on severe inclines, as well as running such a load at high speed is clearly shown. (See C. J. Allen, Railway Magazine January 1958).

Table 4 (Right)
Duchess of Hamilton and a classic run over Shap with 560 tons. Three minutes down at Penrith, time was restored by Tebay and the net time was nearly five minutes under booked time although signal checks caused some loss of time. (See Modern Railways, O. S. Nock January 1962).

Dist.	Engines, 4-6-2 Nos. Load, tons tare Load, tons gross	Sched.	46229 264 275		46229 264 275	
Miles		min.	m. s.	mph	m. s.	mph
0.0	CARLISLE	0	0 00	—	0 00	—
2.0	*Kingsmoor*	—	3 55	—	4 00	50
4.1	*Rockcliffe*	—	5 55	68	6 07	63
6.1	*Floriston*	—	7 36	75	7 55	70
			sigs.	*5	troughs	*56
8.6	*GRETNA*	10	11 26	—	10 30	58
13.0	Kirkpatrick	—	17 58	57/60	14 49	65
			sigs.	70/*25		
16.7	Kirtlebridge	—	22 21	—	18 00	79
20.1	Ecclefechan	—	26 19	58½	20 37	75
22.7	*Castlemilk*	—	28 48	61	22 41	71
25.8	LOCKERBIE	24	31 19	79	25 05	80
28.7	Nethercleugh	—	33 32	80	27 13	84
31.7	Dinwoodie	—	35 50	82/80	29 20	82
34.5	Wamphray	—	37 50	86	31 20	
36.8	*Murthat*	—	—	—	34 00	sig. stop
					35 50	
39.7	BEATTOCK	36	41 51	70½	40 28	63
45.4	*Greskine*	—	48 05	45	46 14	54
49.7	*Summit*	51	54 00	42½	50 57	54
52.6	Elvanfoot	—	56 41	77½	53 26	75/70
55.3	Crawford	—	58 46	75	55 33	78
57.8	Abington	—	60 56	65	57 30	80
60.4	*Wandelmill*	—	63 18	72½	59 25	76
					sigs.	*22
63.2	Lamington	—	65 10	80½	62 42	
66.9	SYMINGTON	—	68 03	73	67 58	55
68.5	Thankerton	—	69 20	80½	69 27	74
70.0	*Leggatfoot*	—	70 31	76½	70 46	*65
73.5	CARSTAIRS	‡73	‡74 43	*17	‡75 45	*12
73.5	Net times (mins.)	73	67½	—	66½	—

* Speed restriction   ‡ Passing time

Engines: Class 8 4-6-2 No. Load: Coaches/tons tare/gross		46229 15/504/560	
Distance		Actual	Speeds
Miles		m. s.	mph
0.00	CARLISLE	0 00	—
1.30	*Carlisle No. 13*	5 18	24
4.90	*Wreay*	12 47	30
7.35	*Southwaite*	17 07	38
10.75	*Calthwaite*	21 55	45
13.05	*Plumpton*	24 48	56
15.60	*Milepost 53½*	27 39	51
17.85	PENRITH	30 01	61
20.10	*Clifton*	34 30	46
24.10	*Milepost 45*	37 27	39
26.15	*Thrimby Grange*	40 42	37/36
27.65	*Harrison's Sidings*	43 11	37
29.35	*Shap*	45 51	38/45
31.40	*Shap Summit*	48 54	37
33.90	*Scout Green*	51 41	70/81
36.90	Tebay	54 03	*65
41.15	*Low Gill*	58 25	50/59
42.95	*Grayrigg*	60 19	53/70
49.95	OXENHOLME	66 34	75
		Sigs.	*35
53.60	*Hincaster Junc.*	70 33	—
55.55	Milnthorpe	72 40	65/68
59.60	*Milepost 9½*	76 17	64
62.80	CARNFORTH	78 51	83
65.95	Hest Bank	81 21	75
69.10	LANCASTER	84 06	66/54
72.10	*Oubeck*	87 10	62
74.80	*Bay Horse*	89 38	68
80.60	Garstang	94 28	76
		Sigs.	*25
85.30	*Barton*	101 15	50
		Sigs.	*25
88.70	*Oxheys*	105 38	—
90.05	PRESTON (pass)	108 36	*25
90.05	Net times (mins.) §	102 15	—

* Speed restriction   § Schedule 107 min.

Table 5.
Some comparisons of work on the southbound climb from Appleby to Ais Gill summit on the Settle and Carlisle line.

Dist		1 14-10-1937 5660 Test Special 9/302/305 425		2 April 1956 46225 Test Special M.T.U. equiv 900 —		3 13-6-64 35012 RCTS Special 9/303/325 470		4 1979§ 40047 Glasgow-Nottingham 9/307/340 473		5 1977§ 47441 WCML Diversion 12/403/425 545		6 1956 "Deltic" Test Special 642 748	
Miles	Run No. Date Engine No. Train Load tons tare/gross Gross train weight	m. s.	mph	m. s.	mph	m. s.	mph	m. s.	mph	m. s.	mph	m. s.	mph
0.00	APPLEBY	0 †00	67	0 †00		0 †00	60	0 00	—	0 †00	57	0 †00	58
2.25	MP 275/Ormside	2 01	77½	2 56	54	2 09	73	3 45	58	2 21	64½	2 15	73
5.25	MP 272/Griseburn					5 05	57	7 10	46½	5 51	47	5 00	56
7.25	MP 270/Crosby Garrett	6 50	58/62½	11 10	37	7 07	68	9 50	56	8 24	53	7 15	64
8.5	MP 268¾												
10.65	KIRKBY STEPHEN	9 56	54	17 16	31½	10 16	61/52	13 34	50	11 53	52	10 25	55/50
13.25	MP 264			Pass						15 02	47½		
14.25	MP 263/Mallerstang	13 58	48/53	Testing		13 47	57/53	—	43/48	15 55	50	14 10	55
16.75	MP 260½			Ended									
17.5	MP 259¾/Ais Gill	18 16	46½			17 46	50	22 36	41	20 29	39	18 10	50
15.25	MP 275-259¾ Average gradient 1 in 124	16 15		—		15 37		18 51		18 08		15 55	

Dist		7 19-3-83 46229 C.M.P. 14/535/560 720		8 23-4-83 46229 Thames-Eden 12/452/480 640		9 30-5-1983 46229 C.M.P. 14/496/530 690		10 5-11-1983 46229 C.M.E. 14/496/530 690		11 7-1-1984 46229 C.M.E. 13/455/485 645	
Miles	Run No. Date Engine No. Train Load tons tare/gross Gross train weight	m. s.	mph	m. s	mph	m. s.	mph	m. s.	mph	m. s.	mph
0.00	APPLEBY	0 00	—	0 00	—	0 00	—	0 00	—	0‡00	—
2.25	MP 275/Ormside	4 24	57	4 11	60	4 21	55	4 23	55/58	3 52	50
5.25	MP 272/Griseburn	7 51	49	7 17	55	8 01	47	7 53	45½	7 33	48
7.25	MP 270/Crosby Garrett	10 18	50	9 24	60	10 28	51	10 32	45½	9 54	53
8.5	MP 268¾	11 51	48	10 37	59/62½	11 55	53	12 10	47½	11 18	55/57
10.65	KIRKBY STEPHEN	14 51	40/44	15 09	2*	14 38	43/45	15 02	40½	13 45	50/48½
13.25	MP 264	18 32	43	21 52	40	18 15	40	18 48	38	16 57	46
14.25	MP 263/Mallerstang	19 50	51	23 11	44/51	19 38	47	20 15	42/48	18 09	53
16.75	MP 260½	22 57	47	24 54	53½	22 46	49½/45	23 45	42½	20 57	53½
17.5	MP 259¾/Ais Gill	23 55	46	26 50	55	23 46	44	24 48	43½	21 49	53
15.25	MP 275-259¾ Average gradient 1 in 124	19 31		22 39		19 25		20 25		17 57	

* Speed restriction   † Passing time   § Year published   ‡ Start from Appleby Dairy (distance .45 miles less)

Run 1 — LMS "Jubilee" class 4-6-0 No. 5660 *Rooke* on a dynamometer car test train. This was an all-out effort from a locomotive in tip-top condition.

Run 2 — *Duchess of Gloucester* on test with the Mobile Test Units set to give an equivalent load of 900 tons. At the low speeds on the bank the cylinder efficiency at long cut-off was not very high. Slipping ended the tests. The engine was worked at 40,000 pounds of steam per hour and 49% cut-off.

Run 3 — Driver Bert Hooker and *United States Lines* on the "Solway Ranger" enthusiasts special. The "Merchant Navy" had the advantage of a flying start but speed dropped up the bank and a minimum of 50 mph at Ais Gill with this load is nothing special.

Run 4 — A packed Glasgow to Nottingham train, running late and worked flat out all the way shows the limitations of these well-loved Type 4s.

Run 5 — Another diesel-electric Type 4 flat out. This time a 47/4 on a diverted WCML express. Speed drops to 39 mph at the summit. Well below "Duchess" capacity.

Run 6 — "Deltic". The prototype with 642 tons of empty stock and a flying start through Appleby. This run shows clearly the ability of this costly machine but the rail horsepower was equalled by 46229 (Run 8) in the acceleration of a total train weight of 640 tons from 2 mph at Kirkby Stephen to 55 mph at Ais Gill Summit.

Run 7 — 46229 on the "Cumbrian Mountain Pullman", plus the "55 Club" set. This was the best steam run since restoration of main line operations by BR.

Run 8 — 46229 on the "Thames-Eden Pullman" going for 'Gold' but foiled by a 31 on the afternoon Carlisle to Leeds service train which had been caught up whilst it was in the long block section between Kirkby Stephen and Garsdale. The acceleration of *Duchess of Hamilton* reflects credit on a supreme effort by the men on the footplate.

Run 9 — 46229 on the "Cumbrian Mountain Pullman", again with the "55 Club" set. This was the best effort to date clipping a few seconds from Run 7.

Run 10 — 46229 on the "Cumbrian Mountain Express" (the SLOA Pullmans had been withdrawn for asbestos-stripping) but still with the "55 Club" Pullmans. The engine was being "run-in" after having piston-valve rings replaced and liners rebored. This was a solid performance.

Run 11 — 46229 on the "Cumbrian Mountain Express" after the engine had been rebored and received new rings to the pistons. This performance, the fastest so far, involved running through drifting snow, blowing off on 1 in 100! and topping Ais Gill at 53 mph minimum with nearly 500 tons trailing load.

A number of speed restrictions due to civil engineering work made these runs unrepeatable until the time of 46229's withdrawal for overhaul. However the line is being improved for increased use so there may be future possibilities for even better runs.

Table 6
Three examples of outputs in excess of 3000 equivalent drawbar horsepower and where cylinder horsepowers would be in the 3500 to 3700 range. In all cases both injectors were on fully and no drop in boiler water level or steam pressure were observed. Indeed as soon as power was reduced blowing off occurred and in no way was performance inhibited on the remainder of the journeys. These are higher than any previous known outputs from a steam locomotive in Britain.

Date	Working	Load (Tons) No./Net/Gross/inc. Loco	Location		Gradient	Acceleration mph
26-5-85	Marylebone-Stratford	11/403/420/580	MP. 19-22	Saunderton	1 in 164	63.4 to 74.6
5-10-85	Marylebone-York	12/435/455/615	MP. 17-20	Saunderton	1 in 164	43.9 to 68.0
26-10-85	Carlisle-York	12/435/460/620	MP. 262-260¼	Mallerstang	1 in 100	28.0 to 47.0

POSTSCRIPT

With the successful arrival in service of the "Coronations" thoughts could turn towards long-term considerations for Anglo-Scottish expresses. Stanier had in fact brought about a situation, in six short years, whereby there was now breathing space in design and development. In 1938 came the first scheme for a possible mechanically-fired streamlined 4-6-4. The grate area was to be 70 sq. ft. and a major concern was for adequate ashpan capacity for working 500 ton trains from Euston to Glasgow on the 6¼ hour "Coronation Scot" timings. The boiler pressure was to be 300 psi and in order to try that pressure in normal service, a batch of "Super Duchesses" was planned with cylinders reduced to 15", further improvements in valve events and streamlined and polished ports and steam passages.

The war ended these and other proposals and wartime batches of Pacifics conformed to the tried and trusted design already in service, the major change being the omission of the streamlined casing for ease of maintenance. The development Office at Derby was closed and many of the staff became involved in Ministry of Supply or other work.

Stanier himself had led a very active engineering life and received the highest of honours from his contemporaries. A member of the Institution of Locomotive Engineers, he was elected its President in 1941 and was conferred with its highest technical award, the James Watt International Medal. He was also a member of the Institution of Locomotive Engineers, its President in 1938 and a recipient of its Gold Medal in 1957. He received a knighthood in 1943 and the following year was elected a Fellow of the Royal Society, only the second locomotive engineer to be so honoured, the first being Robert Stephenson. Sir William officially retired from the LMS in 1944 but was retained by the Company in the capacity of Consultant. He died on 27 September 1965 at the age of 89.

Following Stanier's retirement the CME post went to C.E. Fairburn, formerly the LMS electrical engineer; he was deeply involved in the Company's diesel-electric schemes but died suddenly in October 1945 and H.G. Ivatt took up the reins. Two main line diesel-electrics were in the pipeline and two "Coronations" on order were held back and re-designed to incorporate a number of labour-saving features to increase availability and compare more favourably in trials with the new motive power. These two locomotives Nos. 6256/7 incorporated roller bearings, a new design of drop grate (with Hulson-type rocker bars), hopper ashpan and 5P4 superheater elements which were found to give increased superheat but were not repeated or taken up on the other Pacifics.

It was anticipated that a new type of Class 8 express 4-6-2 would appear as part of the British Railways "Standard" locomotive programme but nothing was done until in 1952, only eight weeks after the former "Turbomotive" had returned to traffic as No. 46202 *Princess Anne*, it was involved in the Harrow & Wealdstone disaster. The decision was made to scrap the engine and replace it with the prototype of a new class.

At an early stage, three cylinders instead of four were specified and following a certain amount of design work on Walschaerts valve gear it was decided to fit British Caprotti poppet valve gear as used on the final two "Black Fives" (Nos. 44686/7). The resulting locomotive - No. 71000 *Duke of Gloucester* - operated from Crewe North shed in the same links as the "Coronation" class Pacifics but it usually worked on

Table 7
Dimensions of contemporary 4-6-2 and 4-6-4 locomotive types for comparison.

Date	Locomotive type	Cylinders (inches)	Driving Wheels (ins)	Boiler pressure (psi)	Grate area (sq. ft.)	Tractive effort (lb. f.)	Adhesion (tons)	Loco in working order (tons)	Loco & full tender (tons)	Maximum height (inches)	Maximum width (inches)	Notes
	Great Britain											
1937	LMS "Coronation" 4-6-2	(4)16.3 × 28	81	250	50.0	40,000	67.0	105.3	161.6	158.0	105.4	4, 5
1946	LNE A-1 4-6-2	(3)19 × 26	80	250	50.0	37,940	66.0	104.1	164.5	157.0	108.0	
1954	BR class 8 4-6-2	(3)18 × 28	74	250	48.6	39,100	66.0	101.3	156.8	156.5	108.0	7, 9
1956	SR rebuilt MN 4-6-2	(3)18 × 24	74	250	48.5	33,495	65.0	97.9	151.4	155.0	105.3	
	France											
1933	Alsace-Lorraine 4-6-2	22.6 × 28.4	76.8	284	48.5	46,000	60.0	106.0	172.0	168.5	122.3	7, 9
1934	Nord (Chapelon) 4-6-2	(2HP16.5 × 25.6 / 2LP25.2 × 27.6)	76.8	246	46.6	47,500	55.9	99.6	177.2	167.3	128.0	1, 4, 8
1949	SNCF 232-U1 4-6-4	(2HP17.6 × 27.6 / 2LP26.8 × 27.6)	78.8	284	55.7	not available	68.0	131.0	211.0	168.5	127.8	1, 2, 4, 9
	Germany											
1935	DRG class 05 4-6-4	(3)17.7 × 26	90.5	284	50.6	33,000	55.4	124.7	209.1	179.1	120.1	4, 5, 9
1957	DB class 10 4-6-2	(3)18.9 × 28.4	78.8	256	42.6	37,037	64.6	117.0	198.0	179.1	120.1	3, 4, 9
	U.S.A.											
1927	PRR K4s 4-6-2	27 × 28	80	205	70.0	44,460	90.0	138.6	237.3	180.0	120.0	2, 4
1937	NYC J3a 4-6-4	22.5 × 29	79	275	81.5	43,440	87.5	160.7	301.0	181.0	125.0	2, 4
1938	Milwaukee F7 4-6-4	23.5 × 30	84	300	96.5	50,300	96.4	185.3	353.1	186.0	126.0	2, 4, 5
1948	C & O L2a 4-6-4	25 × 30	78	255	90.0	52,100	98.0	197.8	374.6	189.5	128.0	2, 6, 7

Notes:
1. Compound expansion
2. Fitted with mechanical stoker
3. Oil burning
4. At least one engine streamlined
5. Types known to have achieved 110 mph"
6. Booster increases starting tractive effort to 66,300 lb.f.
7. Poppet valves
8. Poppet valves (HP only)
9. Only 1 or 2 examples built

The above table shows how the British loading gauge extremely limits the physical size of locomotives. Size for size the LMS "Coronation" class is a world beater. Only the complex and sophisticated Chapelon pacific has an edge, in power:weight terms, but it has the benefit of a much more generous loading gauge. Its maximum output has been approached by 46229 and with fairly modest "tuning" could be surpassed.

the southern half of the route; under the common-user system many crews, due perhaps partly to unfamiliarity with the different techniques needed to drive it, had few good words to say for the engine and the "Coronations" were to remain the final high-power WCML steam design until the diesel onslaught.

Taking into account the limitations of the British loading gauge and axle loadings, and the lack of any experience with mechanical stoking, the design must go down as one of the most successful of all time, standing comparison with those of other companies and countries, some of which are detailed in the accompanying table.

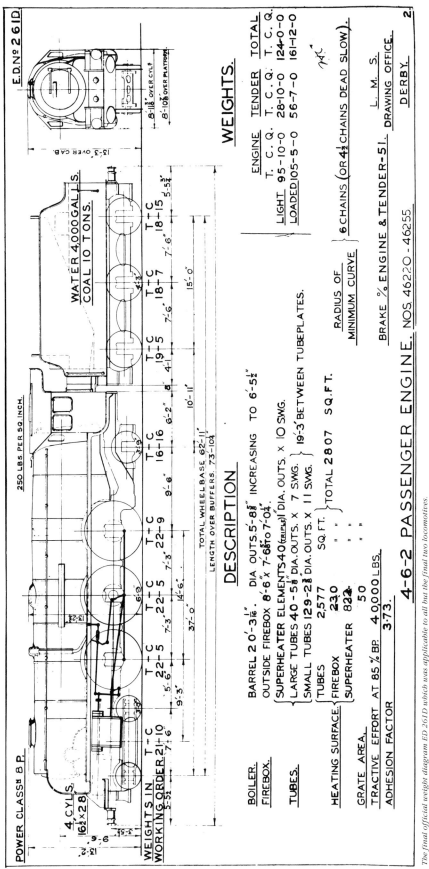

The final official weight diagram ED 261D which was applicable to all but the final two locomotives.

FURTHER READING

For those readers who may have found that they would like to study further some of the topics briefly covered in this book, a selection of recommended books and articles is listed below under relevant subject headings although some references cover many topics. Most of these works should be available through the public library service and the library inter-loans scheme. All are available for reference in the National Railway Museum Library. Potential researchers should write, in the first instance, for a reader's ticket to the Librarian, NRM, Leeman Road, York, YO2 4XJ.

The West Coast Main Line

Charles Lee: "The London and Birmingham Railway", *Railway Magazine Vol. 83 1938(2) pp 255-66, 334-41*.

N. W. Webster: *Joseph Locke: Railway Revolutionary*. (George Allen & Unwin 1970. ISBN 0 04 385055 3)

N. W. Webster: *Britain's First Trunk Line: The Grand Junction Railway*. (Adams & Dart 1972. SBN 2 39 00105 2)

Brian Reed: *Crewe to Carlisle*. (Ian Allan 1969. SBN 7110 0057 3)

Harold D. Bowtell: *Over Shap to Carlisle: the Lancaster and Carlisle Railway in the 20th Century*. (Ian Allan 1983. ISBN 0 7110 1313 6)

Peter Lee: *The Trent Valley Railway (Rugby-Stafford 1847-1966): A Pictorial Record*. (Trent Valley Publications 1988. ISBN 0 948131 15 2)

Geoffrey Kitchenside: *The West Coast Route to Scotland* (David & Charles 1976. ISBN 0 7153 7210 6)

The LMS

Hamilton Ellis: *London Midland & Scottish: A Railway in Retrospect*. (Ian Allan 1970. SBN 7110 0048 4)

O. S. Nock: *A History of the LMS (3 Parts)*. George Allen & Unwin 1982 and 1983)

Michael Bonavia: *The Four Great Railways*. (David & Charles 1980. ISBN 0 7153 7842 2)

Michael Bywater: "Josiah Charles Stamp (1880-1941): Statistician and Railway Company Chairman" in ed. David J. Jeremy *Dictionary of Business Biography Vol 5, S-Z*. (Butterworths 1986. ISBN 0 406 27345 6)

A. J. Pearson: *Man of the Rail*. (Allen & Unwin 1967)

LMS Locomotive Practice

E. S. Cox: *Locomotive Panorama (2 Vols)*. (Ian Allan 1965 and 1966)

E. S. Cox: *Chronicles of Steam*. (Ian Allan 1967)

E. A. Langridge: "Under 10 CMEs". *SLS Journal between Vol. 49, 1973 p.326 and Vol. 65, 1989 p210)*

Sir William Stanier

H. A. V. Bulleid: *Master Builders of Steam*. (Ian Allan 1963)

O. S. Nock: *William Stanier: A Biography*. (Ian Allan 1964)

E. S. Cox: *Speaking of Steam*. (Ian Allan 1971. ISBN 0 7110 0236 3)

LMS Pacifics

John F. Clay and J. Cliffe: *The West Coast Pacifics*. (Ian Allan 1976: ISBN 0 7110 0691 1)

J. W. P. Rowledge: *LMS Pacifics*. (Loco. Profile No. 37, Profile Publications 1974)

ed. Douglas Doherty: *The LMS Duchesses*. (Model & Allied Publications 1973. ISBN 0 85242 325 X)

A.J. Powell: *Stanier Pacifics at Work* (Ian Allan 1986. ISBN 0 7110 1534 1)

J. W. P. Rowledge: *The LMS Pacifics*. (David & Charles 1987. ISBN 0 7153 8776 6)

Trains and Services

Cecil J. Allen (revised B. K. Cooper): *Titled Trains of Great Britain*. 6th ed. Ian Allan 1983. ISBN 0 7110 1309 8)

Clive S. Carter: *Passenger Train Formations 1923-1983; LMS-LM Region*. (Ian Allan 1987. ISBN 0 7110 1606 2)

David Jenkinson: *An Illustrated History of LNWR Coaches (including West Coast Joint Stock)*. (Oxford Publishing Co. 1978. SBN 902888 90 0)

Bob Essery and David Jenkinson: *An Illustrated History of LMS Coaches 1923-1957*. (Oxford Publishing Co. 1977. SBN 902888 83 8)

R. E. Charlewood: "The Midday Scot" in *Trains Annual* (Ian Allan 1950)

Stan Wix: "The Royal Scot in LMS Days" *Railway World 1979 pp. 158-168.*

Duchess of Hamilton

D. H. Ward and F. J. Bellwood: "The Restoration of *Duchess of Hamilton*" *Railway World Vol. 42 1981 pp. 118-126*

Michael Harris: "Putting on the Style: the 55 Club on the main line" *Railway World Vol. 43 1982 pp. 524-6*

G. A. M. Wood: "The Triumphs of *Duchess of Hamilton*" *Railway World Vol. 44 1983 pp. 583-7, 590-1*

Locomotive Running

A. J. Powell: *Living with London Midland Locomotives*. (Ian Allan 1977. ISBN 0 7110 0728 4)

M.F. Higson: *London Midland Fireman*. (Ian Allan SBN 7110 0321 1)

Fred C. Bishop: *Queen Mary of the Iron Road*. (Jarrolds 1946)

Driver L. A. Earl: *Speeding North with the "Royal Scot"* (Oxford University Press 1939)

H. G. Forsyth: *Steam Shed Potrait*. (Atlantic 1981. ISBN 0 9068 990 2 8)

H. G. Forsyth: *Men of Steam: A Portrait of Life on the Footplate*. (Atlantic 1981. ISBN 0 9068 9904 4)

Performance

O. S. Nock: *60 Years of West Coast Express Running*. (Ian Allan 1976. ISBN 0 7110 0618 0)

O. S. Nock: *LMS Steam*. (David & Charles 1971. ISBN 0 7153 5240 7)